THE TREE OF LIFE

H. J. MASSINGHAM

The
TREE
of
LIFE

"True to the Kindred Points of Heaven and Home"

Angelico Press

Cover design
by Michael Schrauzer

PREFACE

THIS book I am aware has many faults : indeed, any of
us who ventures into an unexplored and mysterious
country will have his misadventures and will often
lose his way. The more so as my journey has been as
an ambassador between two countries of the mind which,
if they have not always been at war with each other, have
become widely separated from and at best indifferent
to one another. I set out on this journey because of
my conviction of the need of the one for the other, of
religion to shine once more upon the earth and of
man who dwells thereon and lives thereby not to
forget the stars. I make often a tactless sort of envoy
and I do very definitely come from the earth to the
other kingdom with whose laws and constitution I
am very imperfectly acquainted. In some quarters I
shall accordingly be regarded as an exile from the one
and a stranger to the other. Of this ambiguous and
somewhat anomalous position I am fully aware, so that
it needed a certain hardihood and even rashness to
attempt the journey. But I am sure that in our unhappy
period it has to be made, and so, for want of a better
one, here is my report of it.

I have no doubt in my mind that a powerful new movement is stirring, though as yet unsure of itself, towards
a reconciliation between the religious and the organic
views of life, and it comes both from the Churches and
the ruralists. We earth-men need the sanction of religion
for our efforts to rediscover the true England, which is
independent of "Left" or "Right" and goes behind
the industrial and financial superstructure that has been
jerry-built on top of it. So, some religious bodies are
beginning to reaffirm man's "creaturehood" in a new way.
Not being his design, Creation confronts him with certain

obligations, disciplines and responsibilities in return
for his enjoyment of it. As one of them states : "An
understanding and reverence for the natural pattern
of human living ought to be an outcome of redeeming
grace," and that it is in the land (considered in its widest
sense) that this law or pattern or rhythm of life finds
its most natural expression. Thus, the conservation
of the earth as the source of real wealth in contradistinction from the artificial standards of wealth derived
from finance and industrialism is a vital concern of a
true religious philosophy and a true interpretation
of what I have called in this book the Doctrine of Creation.
The struggle of the future will not be between Left and
Right, between Socialism and a predatory individualism
(as it once was) but between the organic view of life
based on the land and the economic materialism of
progressives, orthodox economists and totalitarians.
Whatever the issue of that struggle, in suspense until
the war is over, let all who truly love our English land
grasp the hand stretched out by this regenerated church-
manship.

In C. E. M. Joad's *God and Evil*, there is during the
course of a debate with Mr. C. S. Lewis a criticism of
the decided weakness of Christian philosophy in respect
of animal life. But the passage in Mr Lewis's *The
Problem of Pain* which Prof. Joad picks out for especial
animadversion is the following : "the goodman-and-the-
good - wife - ruling - their - children - and - their -beasts-in-the
good-home-stead." This, says Prof. Joad, "is parochialism
in *excelsis*" and therefore "in the highest degree unplaus-
ible" because this conception "belongs to the past of
civilization," and "is palpably dying in the present."
Further on, he gives as one of his reasons for rejecting
the divinity of Christ that the claim is "topographically
parochial." "Space is very large, Palestine is comparatively small. Why am I expected to believe that

what happened in Palestine is of such unique importance ?" In this astonishing judgment there can be little doubt that the voice of Joad is that of contemporary secular opinion, and that this is so has been my main urge in writing this book. For it illustrates in a fashion far more revealing than the most devastating criticism of it the root-fallacy of the doctrine of progress, and the enslavement to the time-flux on the one hand and the quantitative assessment of value on the other which it entails. My contention in this book is more than the obvious one that certain values and realities are of permanent significance. The factors that have hindered Prof. Joad from embracing Christianity are the very ones that seem to me of its very essence in the sense that the choice of Bethlehem for the birth-place of Christ into the family of a rural "goodman" was a sign to the world only third in importance to that of the Crucifixion and the Logos. One of the principal reasons for the disintegration of civilization to-day is its neglect of that sign and all its implications. These implications are what I have tried to expound in the book, not because I feel myself qualified to do so, but because this neglect has had such lamentable consequences that it is very necessary for somebody to do it. I need hardly add that I only pick upon Prof. Joad as expressing the prevailing view in a conveniently tabloid form. For the courage of the book from which I have taken the above passages, the courage of *unlearning*, I have nothing but admiration.

In conclusion, I would wish to acknowledge my great indebtedness to my friends, Mr M. B. Reckitt and Mr Willoughby Dewar, who did me the honour of reading the MS. and purging it of not a few errors.

December, 1942.   H. J. M.

CONTENTS

Chapter   Page
PREFACE 6
I. HEAVEN AND EARTH 11
   I. The Conquest of Religion . . . 12
   II. The Conquest of Nature . . . 13
   III. The Kinship between Them . . . 14
   IV. A New Religion? 16

II. THE RURAL CHRIST 18
   I. Peasant Galilee and the Roman Slave-
      Farms 18
   II. The Rural Redeemer 21
   III. The Peasant Poetry of the Gospels . 24
   IV. The Peasant Prince of Peace . . 25
   V. The Christ of the Trades . . . 28
   VI. The Christian-Pagan Christmas . . 29

III. THE BRITISH CHURCH 33
   I. A Religious Friendship with Nature . 33
   II. The Interplay of Nature, Art and
      Religion 38
   III. The Native Independence of the Western
      Church 42
   IV. The Husbandry of the Wilds . . 46

IV. THE MIDDLE AGES AND THE NATURAL LAW . 52
   I. The Rise and Fall of the Cistercians . 52
   II. The Religious Change towards Nature . 56
   III. The Peasantry and Power-Politics . 58
   IV. The Concept of the Natural Law . . 63
   V. Natural Satanism 67

V. THE RECOVERY OF THE 17TH CENTURY . . 74
   I. The Age of Reconciliation . . . 74
   II. The Poets and the Natural Creation . 78
   III. Nature and Christianity in Shakespeare
      and Browne 85
   IV. The Same in Milton and the Cambridge
      Platonists 90
   V. Heaven and Earth in the 17th Century . 95

9

Chapter		Page
VI.	THE SEPARATION OF NATURE FROM RELIGION	101
	I. Nature as the Great Machine	101
	II. Locke's Idea of Nature *v.* Shakespeare's	104
	III. The "Natural Law" of Hobbes and Descartes	108
	IV. Spengler's, Hardy's and Huxley's Idea of Nature *v.* Shakespeare's	114
	V. Nature as Anarchy and Mechanism	123
	VI. The Apostasy of the Churches	127
VII.	THE DECLINE OF THE PEASANTRY	130
	I. The Permanent Peasant Values	130
	II. Changeless Craftsmanship	137
	III. The Pillars of Society Pulled Down	139
	IV. The Sterilization of Nature	143
	V. The Degradation of Work	151
	VI. The Degradation of Property	153
VIII.	ENQUIRY INTO NATURE	159
	I. Shakespeare and the Misuse of Free Will	159
	II. Not in Our Stars	162
	III. Nature Acquitted	169
	IV. The Renaissance Exhausted in Our Time	173
	V. The Person, Nature and the Machine	177
IX.	THE DOCTRINE OF CREATION	180
	I. Doctrine and the Modern World	180
	II. Doctrine *v.* Puritanism	182
	III. Shakespeare and the Sense of Sin	186
	IV. The Unity of Nature and Religion	189
X.	THE CHURCH ACROSS THE FIELDS	193
	I. Church and Creation	193
	II. The Recovery of the English Tradition	199
	III. Alternative to Modernism	203
	IV. The Rebirth of England	208
INDEX		212

CHAPTER ONE

HEAVEN AND EARTH

"I feel that the loss of the love of the land for its own sake and the loss of the Christian religion are the greatest tragedies this country has ever suffered."

THIS is an extract from a letter to me written by a naval lieutenant and it is the theme of this book. The profound truth of these words could not be more simply expressed. This dual loss[1] is the real cause of our own tribulation and of our impotence to extract ourselves from it. It is the cause of the "Decline of the West." And, since it is a dual cause and that the tragedy cannot be accounted for by the one without the other, I propose to examine whether they are related, how they are related and by what means they can be reintegrated in practice, and in our consciousness.

No study could be more formidable. The theme is not only vast and embarrassingly elusive, but its obscurity covers both definition and materials. Moreover, the modern world has drifted so far away from Christianity and Nature alike that few of those who call themselves Christian perceive any necessary connection between them, while even the wisest of those who advocate a new organic way of living as a means of arresting the rapid decline of civilization content themselves with the vague and pious aspiration that the revival of rural values should be "spiritual" no less than practical and cultural. Yet the right name for Western civilization is surely Western Christendom; it is a definitely Christian culture and any attempt to indicate lines of rescue from

---

[1] The approach to a purely secular society has been extraordinarily rapid in the 20th century.

11

its present *descensus Averni* must recognize the Christian actualities of the origins and growth from which it has so widely departed. It was in fact my own recognition that modern Christendom is now divorced alike from the soil and its own historical genesis that induced me to nerve myself for the task of exploring the historical warrants of their reunion. My conviction that our civilization is collapsing for need of these foundations to its structure was not in the long run to be deterred by my own signal lack of qualifications for undertaking such a task.

I. *The Conquest of Religion.*

There is another serious impediment to this study which is at the same time an inducement to pursue it. Excepting in odd corners of the social edifice, neither the Christian Faith nor the natural faith are what they once were. The Faith reached its lowest decline between about 1750 and 1830, a period corresponding with that of the Enclosures from which the clergy exorbitantly benefited. From that time forward it has been slowly and painfully finding its way back from the churchyard to the church. The faith, on the other hand, has sunk lower and lower until brusque Necessity has forced us to recognize that we cannot live without it. Christians, wrote R. H. Tawney in *The Acquisitive Society*, are "a small sect in a pagan society." But society is not even pagan, it is secular, which is a very different thing. Pagan society was full of natural faith, even when it took the quasi-modern form of Cæsarism in the Emperor Cult of the Roman Empire. "A society," wrote Tawney in the same book,

> "whose Founder was executed as the enemy of law and order need not seek to soften the materialism of principalities and powers with mild doses of piety administered in an apologetic whisper."

But that is exactly what it has done. "The abdication by the Christian Churches," wrote the same author,

> "of one whole department of life, that of social and political life as the sphere of the powers of this world and of them alone, is one of the capital revolutions through which human society has passed. The Churches of the 19th century . . . acquiesced in the popular assumption that the acquisition of riches was the main end of man, and confined themselves to preaching such personal virtues as did not conflict with its achievement."

If Christianity had paid even lip-service to Cæsar between the first and fifth centuries A.D., an apologetic whisper would certainly not have carried its voice to the Ultima Thule of the British Isles. The abdication, that is to say, has not only affected the response to Christianity of the external world but the quality and inspiration of the Faith itself.[1]

II. The Conquest of Nature.

The same disintegration has befallen the human attitude to nature. Modern civilization having become urban in culture, government, industry and habitation, the approach to nature has been revolutionized accordingly. The mediæval "law of nature" has given way to the Darwinian "conquest of nature," which means conquering nature by nature's own presumed prescriptions. This policy of aggression impoverished natural fauna, vegetation, fertility and resources to such an extent that neither wild nor domesticated nature is anything like so rich as it once was. Nature's plenty is rapidly becoming wishful thinking. The wild lands in their teeming fecundity have become more and more barren ; the lands

[1] The Nazi and Communist State-religions have, of course, been attempts to fill the abhorred vacuum. Our own "Left" is going in the same direction.

populated by man more and more suburban. In our own day the process has reached its culmination by the increasing industrialization of actual farming land, and the application of new laws and methods of the inorganic to animate germination, growth, rhythms and associations. The old symbiosis between land and people is almost extinct and the old "law of nature," persistent through all adversity in our own people, is to-day almost solely nostalgic and reminiscent. Even primordial sex has passed on from the Pervigilium Veneris to the laboratory. Chemistry is the dictator of the organism ; cash of cropping ; measurement of life ; finance of the farm. Food comes not from the fields but from the factory ; and thought is denatured as well as food. Houses are pre-fabricated and owe nothing to rock, soil or timber. Our native earth was once our home ; then it became our recreation ; now it is a business like any other industry, not a livelihood. Distance has become a value in itself by the obsolescence of the home-sense. The horizon rules our affairs, not the threshold and internationalism is the new word for neighbourliness. The concrete, the realistic and the empirical are replaced by the abstract and the schematic, while the natural stuff of life is regarded as machinery to be ruled and regulated by machinery. Nature's family—father, mother, child—is merged into the atomic mass and the replacement of regional by centralized forces logically follows.

III. The Kinship between Them.

These are some of the many aspects of modern life which run contrary to man's natural inheritance, and they are becoming so masterful and omnipresent that one acquainted with them but not with the history of animate nature might well conclude that animal life was the product of the retort and the test-tube rather than of the ovum and the uterus. The first analogy, therefore between Christianity and Nature is that both, assumed to be temporary phases of attachment through which a progressive humanity has passed, subjective anachronisms rather than objective presentations of eternal truths, have shrunk in human valuation and fallen into a decline. That does not mean, of course, that there is any closer relation between them ; it only means that they are companions in neglect, misfortune and poverty. What is significant is that Western civilization has declined with them and it is only a step thence that, just as they have lost by Western civilization abandoning them, so Western civilization has lost in the act of abandonment. For when man lived more or less naturally, and at the same time believed the world to be the porch to an other-worldly room, his civilization made rapid and intensive growth, whereas he has made a sufficiently poor job of his own self-glorification in disowning Mother Earth and the Fatherhood of God.

If they are related to him in terms of his well-being and estranged from him in terms of his sickness, what, if any, are the terms by which they are related to one another ? As I have said, the regenerative forces in contemporary society which plead for an organic or Christian way of life are even fewer than their fewness when they plead for both in unison. There are, in fact, only two methods whereby that unity in truth may be discovered. One is the historical method, that of examining the past from its Christian origins onwards for evidences of harmony between Christian and natural values ; the other is equally historical but confined to the phenomena of the 20th century, in which the repudiation of the first is seen to implicate the repudiation of the second and *vice versa*, while the consequences are the same in each. This study, if successful, leads to the conclusion that civilized man and indeed man himself, whether civilized or savage or as he is to-day civilized-savage, cannot survive without a reaffirmation of Christian realities in harmony with natural ones.   Into what form or forms the harmony should shape itself is the province of speculation rather than of empiricism and necessarily tentative in exposition.   It should round off and close the previous enquiries.

IV. A New Religion ?

But, it may be asked—granted man's need for religion, to worship something other than himself for the recovery of his sanity and health, and his very dangerous alienation from natural law which experience may well be proving not to be identical with what is called "the law of the jungle," why not a new religion, a purely humanist one that will regard man as the evolutionary product of nature ? The answer surely is that man does so regard himself already.   This concept is not a religious one at all and humanism has already been tried and found wanting.   History clearly demonstrates that mankind must worship something, if not the Christian Trinity, then himself or the State or a particular "race" of his own or some extra-cosmic Absolute or Nature as his pagan ancestors did or the abstract gospel according to Marx or the pantheist "world-soul."   There is nothing new in any of them and all are either immanent or trans-cendental, none are both.   The essence of Christianity is that it *is* both and that its whole philosophy was framed upon the interaction between them.

But, the dialectic proceeds, if none of these have availed to secure man from self-destruction and the disintegration both of his person and his society, has Christianity fared the better ? Thus once more we are brought up with a demand for a historical retrospect, since Christianity would not have supplanted Paganism

16

if its nature-worship had been true to the nature and adequate to the needs of Western man, while only history can show the dividing line when Christendom began to depart from Christianity, and to what extent the embryonic causes of that division have developed into the anarchic consequences of the 20th century. Nor can the Christian Faith (seeing that there is no alternative to it) itself be rejuvenated unless it be equally shown that its own division from nature has pauperized it as an all-sufficient gospel for modern, grown-up, Western man, wrecked in the bitter sea of his delusion of self-will. The pagan story of the Tree Iggdrasil, the Tree of Life, whose roots were in earth and topmost branches in heaven, prefigures that gospel.

It is proper then to begin with the Figure from which Christendom itself began, and in whom the transcendental, the immanent and the natural are perfectly reconciled.

CHAPTER TWO

THE RURAL CHRIST

I. Peasant Galilee and the Roman Slave Farms.

THE end of the life of Christ has overshadowed the beginning, yet his birth in a manger at Bethlehem is of immeasurable significance as a symbol of the human relationship to nature. The King of Kings was born in a village cow-byre : even if the tale were but legendary, the immensity of the paradox is a revelation of ultimate truth. If the birth of Christ be the meeting of man and God, the farmyard is the meeting-place of man with nature. But in case dull man should miss the enormous meaning rising from this simplicity like the djinn out of the bottle, the paradox is heavily underlined. The birth in the manger is not an adventure story of highness in lowliness, like the many tales of classical antiquity or Indian and other mythologies where the demigod or hero, Hercules for instance, is dispossessed of his true estate, is placed in bondage, performs menial tasks and is forced to hide his identity in an environment of test and hardship not natural to his exalted position. On the contrary, the farmyard setting of the infant Christ is not only natural but organic ; his mother is a peasant married to the village carpenter. Homage is paid him in Luke by unlettered shepherds "keeping watch on their flocks by night" and in Matthew by the Magi, the repositories of learning and wisdom in the Syriac culture, as though by pictorial illustration to draw together the two extremes of labour in the fields and transcendental kingship, the heavens and the earth, the base of the

18

pyramid of human society and the apex. It is hardly
fanciful to add that these two extremes are not only
drawn together but fused in the words of St Chrysostom :
"God has placed man in a royal palace, more wonderful
than any palace."

But the paradox would lose much of its power if the
birth of Christ had occurred and his boyhood and early
manhood had been lived in the membership of a peasant-
craftsman's household in a village and remote countryside,
whose conditions had been normal to the Romano-
Syriac world. But the Bethlehem region was quite
definitely a rural area of peasant population within the
orbit of a highly sophisticated and urbanized world
which had seen the full development of the Hellenic city-
state. More, the city-state had already passed its
meridian and was entering upon the first phase of its
eclipse by way of that Cæsarism which Christianity was
to repudiate and Toynbee in his monumental *Study of
History* has called the age of the Dominant Minority.
The cosmopolitan Roman Imperium was breaking down
the regional self-government of its provinces by the
machinery of an economic oppression which enriched the
urban plutocracy of the Empire at the expense of those
provinces. The Cæsarean despotism may well have been
responsible for the execution of Christ by his refusal to
be the Messiah of an armed insurrection against it and
the recoil of the nationalist populace of Jerusalem,
headed by the priesthood, against him on that account.

But the political aspects of Roman urbanism are less
to the purpose here than the economic transformation of
the provincial Empire by the policy of large-scale corn-
production at its perimeter to feed the urbanized masses
of the Roman proletariat. The exploitation of Asia
and Africa (and in later times Britain) in the interests
of this large-scale specialized agriculture and by means
of the villa-system and its gangs of slave-labourers

could not but disorganize the peasant system of subsistence farming and the peasant values associated with
it. Then, as now, an autocratic central government
proved compatible with the vested interests of the corn
merchant and the shipping magnate, and the provincial
cities gradually forfeited their original control and
initiative. The practice of farming out the customs was
rife in Judæa. In this expansion Rome was only repeating
her own previous course of action with the Italian
peasantry which had made her great during the Republic.
Agrarian revolution on behalf of urban capitalism, so
strenuously and unavailingly opposed by Tiberius
Gracchus and his brother, is paralleled by the 18th to
19th century Enclosures on behalf of urban capitalism
in our own country, so strenuously and unavailingly
opposed by Cobbett. The fruits of both movements
was the destruction of the peasantry. *Latifundia perdidere Italiam:* Enclosure turned English peasants into
paupers.

This historical clash between the country and the town,
between a stable peasantry and the factory-villa of a
landless slave-labour, between the mixed farm raising
food for home consumption and monoculture for the
mass-production of grain and the export of cheap food
for the urban masses, was acute during the lifetime
of Christ in Judæa. Yet it is rarely if ever brought
into relevant contact and contrast with the matrix, the
atmosphere and the incidents of that life. If the divinity
of Christ be accepted, the choice of his earthly habitation
is of supreme and symbolic moment. As his place was
retired from the centres of the autumnal Hellenistic-
Syriac civilization, in like manner was his mission detached
from the political ferment of that uneasy captive of
Leviathan whose smouldering discontents were to end
in abortive revolt and the sack of Jerusalem by the
soldiers of Titus. The eternal "I AM" made his temporary

home with the most immemorial of all human settlers upon the cultivated earth since man had left his primitive childhood, the least subject to the stresses and strains of States and the fluctuations of empire—the peasantry. He made his home among the great home-makers of all civilized nations in all periods, and who alone maintain that personal intimacy with the earth from which one civilization after another releases itself to its final destruction.

The Incarnation indeed sheds a heavenly light upon all those peasant peoples who form the walls and pillars of the great human family under the fatherhood of God and whose microcosm is the Holy Family. Recent anthropology has traced the origins of the human community not to the tribal but the family unit—a tribe is in essence a cluster of households—while the borderline between primitive and peasant is also crossed by the chosen household in Bethlehem being that of a village craftsman. For craftsmanship antedates husbandry and our first knowledge not only of Homo but Homunculus is as a craftsman. With the discovery of agriculture the rural crafts gathered as satellites round the solar and sovereign craft of husbandry, multiplied and swung round its magnetic attraction. Or, to put it in more organic terms, craftsmanship, once the root which grew the trunk of husbandry, itself became the proliferating branches in intimate dependence upon the trunk. It is not straining meaning out of the true to speak of the sacred Dove descending to settle among the branches of that Tree.

II. The Rural Redeemer.

If the village birth and upbringing of Christ be mythological, the record of his mission is unaccountable. His journeyings were so completely those of a countryman,

21

his associations so obviously rural, his followers so clearly drawn from small market towns and villages and his own concrete and pictorial methods of expression so fundamentally a peasant speech transfigured that, if he was not actually born in a manger and visited by shepherds, it would have been necessary to have invented that he did. His debt to his native soil was indeed far more explicitly expressed than Shakespeare's, on whose work the stamp of country England was incomparably more sharply and indelibly impressed than it was on any of his contemporary dramatists. Shakespeare actually spent the best years of his life in the capital, Christ never entered it except on seasonal occasions and to mark the apotheosis of his earthly visitation. The principal city of Galilee among the many girdling the lake-shore, the Hellenistic Tiberias, built by the tetrarch, Herod Antipas, and so disfavoured by the Jews, is never so much as mentioned in the Gospels. There is no record of Christ having even entered the other Hellenized cities like Bethsaida or Cæsarea Philippi, the seat of the Roman procurator and the hive of the tax-gatherers. He remained a regional figure and there was not the faintest veneer of cosmopolitan culture either in his life or his utterances. It was the multitudes who came to him in the country, not he who went to the multitudes in the town. Indeed, he is represented as taking refuge from crowd-scenes on shipboard, up mountain and in garden, and it was a retired garden which was the place of the agony of the last days.

Perhaps it is because only a small minority in an industrial civilization is country-minded that the sublimated peasant poetry of Christ is not recognized as what it is. Yet the subject-matter of the Discourses and Parables is pronouncedly rural and regional. The references to husbandry and the round of the seasons are so numerous that Dr Gore in his *Jesus of Nazareth* infers from them a countryside of "owners of large properties with their stewards and servants and hired labourers" encroaching on native settlements of "householders possessing small holdings and living on their own produce." That bears out my previous statements that the remoter provinces of the early Empire were witnessing a centrifugal movement of the *latifundia* into the lands of the local peasantry.

But it is legitimate to go a good deal further than the bare pointer of the Parables constantly drawing the materials of their graphic analogies, illustrations, similes, and narrative examples from the home-life of the Galilean peasantry—the village, the fields and the workshop. The whole atmosphere of them is one of country craftsmanship, and Jewish documents do actually reveal that Galilee was a region particularly rich in country industries. The Parables are indeed saturated in ruralism, using the commonest experiences of home-keeping man to throw a blinding light upon universal truths, infinite realities. There could not be a more telling example of Blake's eternity in a grain of sand, of the sky seen in the raindrop, the universal in the particular, the mustard tree in the mustard seed and the whole in the part. Dr Gore himself remarks that they

> "appear to be based upon a deep principle—that any 'law of nature' and anything fundamentally characteristic of human conduct (even in bad men) is a revelation of the divine. God and his ways are to be looked for in nature and in anything fundamentally human."

It is time indeed that this country-mindedness of a few living in a pocket of an urbanized world of capitalist farming, when far lands were being exploited for the *panem et circenses* of Imperial cities, should be sharply apprehended by a contemporary world for whom the agricultural issue has become more insistent and peremptory than ever before in the world's history.

III. The Peasant Poetry of the Gospels.

But the rural substance of the speech of Christ goes beyond its reflection of an agricultural community, just as its psychology goes beyond ethics. It is also a country speech in texture, form and mode of thought. It is a concrete, domestic, realistic poetry, the very reverse of that intellectual abstraction which is town-bred. Thus, whether it be hortatory or mystical or dialectical, it does not desert the field-path of familiar narrative, based on observation and experience. It is a tale-telling poetry like that of Chaucer and John Clare, and over and over again it is proverbial, as Shakespeare's frequently is. Yet, as T. R. Glover has justly pointed out in *The Conflict of Religions in the Early Roman Empire*, it is never fabular in the Æsop manner, but considers animals and plants as they really are—under the providence of God. The clucking hen, the worried flock, the plough-ox, the fallen sparrow and the lost sheep, are symbolized without ceasing to be natural. To *consider* the lilies of the field in the sense of appreciating what Raleigh called the "peculiar virtue and operation" of living things is in a profound sense the naturalist's point of view, and it is clear how antipathetic such directness of mind must have found the hyprocrisy, sophistication and external mummeries of the Pharisees. The appeal is not to authority but the reality of experience. This open-air speech is, too, oral, like all peasant literature, and traditional as home-speech handed down from generation to generation invariably is. As such it is the supreme example, dealing as it does with the well-worn coinage of maxim, proverb and aphorism, of the compatibility between tradition and the utmost range of originality. Dr Gore remarks upon Dr Burney's analysis of the technical frame of Christ's teaching as the "parallelism" of rhythmical couplets or triplets or four-lined stanzas, either "synthetic" or antithetic,

This is not merely the device of Hebraic poetry but one form out of many such forms by which peasant rhythms keep peasant memory intact.

The life of the earth and of man's tillage of it breathes so deeply and rhythmically through the very pores of this patterned poetry that beside it the set rituals of the nature-gods of the ancients seem hardly more than external mechanisms, a necessary binding of the community life but not a spiritual integration between man and nature. We gather from them a rich sense of the systole and diastole of the seasonal round, we are partakers in the cyclical motion of ebb and flow, but the poetic downrightness of the carpenter's bench, of the fisherman's boat, of leavening meal, of the impartial rain falling on all alike, of God clothing the grass of the field as by the swing of the sower's arm, of the ears of corn plucked on a Sunday in defiance of man's servitude to institutions, this realism, this inwardness of meaning, are absent from the pagan religions. The Nature-God of the Gospels is so in an entirely new way—"our God is the God of Nature," as Tertullian said—; we see in his Logos ·a sacramentalism not in the celebration of the great natural mysteries but in the daily task of craftsman and husbandman under the paternal eye that is now more than the sun. A new twist has been given to man's communion with the Creation.

IV. The Peasant Prince of Peace.

Yet the archaic symbolism of natural rite and festival is not discarded—else had the Christian pilgrims never have captured the strongholds of Paganism. It is implicit in the informal ceremony of the Last Supper, wherein the unity between nature and the new faith is expressed in the sacramental aspect of the bread and the wheat, the body of the heavenly visitant, as Osiris of old was represented as the ear of barley. So "I am the true Vine" and the host of images associated with it are not merely natural images to express spiritual truths. They are the Christian consummation of the Dionysian mysteries, just as Traherne's "orient and immortal wheat" is another translation of the same concept. It appears again in Nicolas Berdyaev's—

> "There are two symbols, bread and money ; and there are two mysteries, the eucharistic mystery of bread and the satanic mystery of money. We are faced with a great task ; to overthrow the rule of money and to establish in its place the rule of bread. Money divorces spirit and world, spirit and bread, spirit and labour. In the symbol of bread spirit becomes one with the flesh of the world. It is completely wrong to base the spiritual life on the old antithesis of spirit and flesh."

One of the distinctive milestones of the relapse of Christendom from Christianity not into Paganism but the nihilism of money was the separation in 1875 of the wheat-germ from the grain by the American steel roller mills. Until it is natural for man to think once more of the field of corn as part of the sacrament of bread, the religious can never be reunited with the organic view of life. The triune relationship of the good earth, the good husbandman and heaven over all is truly contained in the life of Christ, the apotheosis of those vegetation deities who was the Village Redeemer and declared himself the Vine of a new fruitfulness. When the sun gilds the field of ripening wheat, we are witnessing year by year a symbol of the Incarnation.

There is a further aspect of the peasant Christ which is rarely noticed by a modern way of thought which has diverged from both peasant and Christian values. In various parts of the last three volumes of his *Study of History*, Dr Toynbee devotes many pages not only to militarism as one of the most direct causes for the extinction of one civilization after another, but to the futility of armed revolts (so frequently repeated by Maccabee and Zealot) against the persecution or oppression of subject peoples or classes by the "Dominant Minority." Against them all he places the immortal scene in the Garden of Gethsemane when Peter resists the arrest of his Master, while the renowned words "Put up thy sword" forms the pivot of his whole elaborate retrospect upon the particular theme of organized violence in the history of nations. In *The Age of the Gods*, Christopher Dawson has written as follows :

> "The earlier changes of culture in Europe have been predominantly peaceful. There is no sign that the transition from the palæolithic to the neolithic age and the expansion of peasant culture in Eastern and Central Europe, even the beginnings of the age of metal in the Mediterranean, were due in any degree to warlike invasions. In fact, from their open settlements and the lack of weapons, war can have played little part in the life of the neolithic peasant peoples. Even in modern times . . . the most primitive peoples, the food-gatherers, are predominantly peaceful."

Dr Marett, in *Psychology and Folk Lore*, writes : "The ethics of amity belong to the natural and normal mood." In most primitive religions, he adds, death is outbalanced by birth, loss by renewal, while the moral always comes before the mechanical. For all its folly and ignorance, the religious world of the savage is a single whole. W. J. Perry has embarked upon a similar research which can leave no real doubt that the neo-Darwinian view of the pugnacity of primitive man is a complete fallacy. The peasant community, of course, is nearer to the primitive than any other, so that the appellation of the Son of Man as the Prince of Peace is organically relevant to his birth from and life within a peasant society. There is more than a poetic significance in Henry Vaughan's—

27

The Tree of Life

"There above strife and danger
Sweet Peace sits crowned with smiles,
And One born in a manger
Commands the beauteous files."

V. The Christ of the Trades.

It is only since the Enclosures and the Industrial Revolution that the idea, the symbol and the actuality of the peasant Christ have receded into the mists of an "obsolete" past, among Christians (with a handful of exceptions), rationalists and indifferentists alike. But that is certainly not true of the Middle Ages, of which the village commoners and the Craft Guilds were the pillars and arches, and the Cistercian Brotherhood part of the vaulting. It is certainly not true of *Piers Plowman* nor of Chaucer's *Povre Persoun.*

Piers Plowman, though by no means Wycliffite and a forerunner of Puritanism, has an element of asceticism in conformity with *Everyman* and other channels of mediæval thought which looked upon the Gospel teaching as a renunciation, not a rebirth, or, as Berdyaev has written, "The Gospel is the glad tidings of the coming of the Kingdom of God rather than an ascetic manual for the salvation of the soul." But John Langland never for one moment lost touch with the peasant springs of the great river of Christendom. I may be permitted here to quote a few lines from my *English Countryman* upon the English rendering of the "Good Shepherd" who was the most representative figure in the early Christian art of the Catacombs.

"In *Piers Plowman* the peasant Christ takes on a definitely Anglicized form : Piers Plowman is conceived as the peasant Messiah . . . for Langland the ploughman was the symbol of a divine humanity whom he actually identified with the divine Craftsman. . . . The plough-

28

man with his vocation was the guardian of the Christian
Faith and the pillar of all true civilization—Piers Plowman
tilleth for all. . . . As S. B. James puts it in *Back to
Langland*, the ideal peasant was the Son of Man. So
Christ and Piers were mystically identified and 'God
speed the Plough' acquires a spiritual profundity in
his pages that goes beyond Bunyan's idea of the New
Faith as embodied in the valiant person of Christian.
Christian was the true Christian, but Piers Plowman the
'Christ of the Trades.'"

Piers Plowman was an attempt to combine the mysticism
with the homiliness of the Incarnation.

So the "Christ of the Trades," a 15th century mural
painting in Breage Church, Cornwall, is at once a literal
and a symbolic translation of the actual Christ who was
a family apprentice to the carpenter's bench of the
village where he was born. A mural at West Chillington,
Sussex, actually paints him so, with roughened hands,
a Sussex waggon-wheel at his feet and as aureole round
his head a chisel, adze, auger and beetle. The peasant
knew what the wise men missed.

VI. The Christian-Pagan Christmas.

The mediæval festival of Christmas was a faithful
rendering of the lily of Christ rising from a pagan compost
of many centuries' growth. The Jewish background of
a rigid monotheism was totally ignored, but not so the
pagan folklore and mythology that cradled the stern
concept of Jehovah. The carol, originally a dance-
cum-song whose Western vogue was set in motion by
St Francis and his disciple, Jacopo da Todi, is far more
authentically rural in scene and incident than any of
the long processions of Arcadias. In one, the offerings
of the shepherds to the sacred burden of the manger
are a lamb, a dog and garden produce in home-made

baskets ; in another, a bell, a flask, a spoon, a pipe and a nuthook are laid upon the floor of the byre. The carnal or carrion crow jubilantly talks over the glad tidings with the crane ; the Babe in the womb bids the cherries lean down for his mother to eat ; the Babe is beaten with a green withy ; the Child brings sowing and harvest within the measure of a single day to beguile Herod's baby-killers, and the gipsies play the part of the Three Kings and tell the fortunes of the Holy Family. So Latin canticles like *Dies est Leatitiæ* and *Quem pastores laudavere* caught the joyful infection from Jack-on-the-Green.

The Nativity Plays, performed by the Craft Guilds on moveable stages in the open air, were as naturally and traditionally rustic as the carols, all the cycles being opened by the choir-boys chanting "Glory to God in the Highest," and the shepherds replying, "Peace on earth to men of good will." In the Wakefield Cycle, a gossiping party of shepherds, a true buffooning misericord, is broken upon by the angel who cries, "Rise, herdsmen hynde ; for now is He born." In the York Cycle, the name of Christ is "Fairest of felde folk," echoing or echoed by the first line of *Piers Plowman*. St Francis, whose little brothers brought the Christmas Crib to the West, was also, it seems, responsible for awakening it to what even Thomas Hardy, the great apostle of "Necessitation Sways," hardly thought to be a legend—the cattle falling on their knees at midnight on Christmas Eve and the bees singing in their hives. It was in honour equally of St Francis, the Christian animist, who said of the birds :

> "God made you noble among creatures, prepared your mansion in the purity of air, and, though you neither sow nor reap, nevertheless without any solicitation on your part, he protects and guides you."

—it was in honour not only of him, but of their archaic corn-goddess that the peasants of Finland hung a sheaf of corn at the gable-end of the farmhouse on Christmas Eve so that the birds thus blest might share in the Festival of Humanity. Thus the glorification of the Galilean village as the home of the Heavenly King was remembered in true historical continuity by the villagers of a whole continent and more than sixty generations.

Yet in the peasants' fathomless folk-memory, this happy recognition of a Nature-God who sought to make an Eden of men's souls made room for the attendants that had paved the way for him, and blended the Festival of the New-Born King with the Festival of the New-Born Year. The Yule Log and the Yule Tree Iggdrasil were as much part of the memorial furniture as the Christmas Tree. The Yule Firth, the Lord of Misrule and the Feast of Fools, when the order of society was inverted and John Nameless took the place of his master, followed on the heels of the shepherds who followed the Eastern Star. The Golden Age of Hesiod and Chronos, liberated from time, joined the Festival that marked the liberation of men from death and sin. The redemption of mankind was linked with the rejuvenation of nature. This was the reason why the Puritans hated Christmas and tried to abolish it. But we whose teeth have been set on edge by inheriting the economic fruits of Puritanism begin dimly to apprehend a universal truth in the Creation, gods and angels, beasts and birds and trees, man and nature, participating in the birthday of the Saviour.

In the capacious store-room of the peasants' memory the fictitious nature-gods were the servants of the one Master. For they, Attis, Zagreus, Osiris, Tammuz, Adonis and Balder, were but gods or deified princes; this one, the supreme God, entered the world to become a peasant like themselves. If it was no accident that Christ was born a Jew from a nation whose office was to purify itself from the idolatries and blood-sacrifice of

31

a *false* nature-cult, it was also no accident that he was born a peasant. The old gods and corn-spirits died at the autumn harvest because only by the death of the year can the spring be reborn. But this One died that all men might share with him the eternal spring of the Commonwealth of God.

CHAPTER THREE

THE BRITISH CHURCH

I. A Religious Friendship with Nature.

"IONA did for England," wrote Helen Waddell in *The Desert Fathers*, "what the Roman Augustine failed to do." It is, I think, more than speculation which discovers the origins of our native love of nature and animals which has distinguished us from all other European peoples, even when it may be violated or perverted, in the British Church which evangelized the extreme West between about A.D. 200 and 700. Where else could it have come from ? The Scandinavian Nordics ? In part, perhaps, that is to say, in receptivity, an openness towards the gentle passion but rough and raw, a kind of brutish love for brutes, until it came into contact with the highly developed, mature and mystical communion with nature of the Christianized Celts. Perhaps it was the blend which produced that paradoxical compatibility between loving the animal and baiting bear or bull, praising birds and caging or collecting them, creating a nature poetry and prose overwhelmingly superior to and more copious than that of any other people in the world's history and destroying the land that inspired it.

This, surely, was one thing Iona did for England. Where and when and how the British Church arose is hidden in the shadows of the Dark Ages, pierced by its radiance, but it must certainly have been before the military and economic domination of Rome had ebbed. It must have taken root when the amphitheatres at Dorchester, Caerleon and Silchester echoed with the

33

shouts of men and the roars of beasts, dying and victorious. Beasts and warriors or captives were fighting in one part of the country, beasts and saints fraternizing in another. The contrast is the reflection of another, that between the Roman *villa-latifundia* with their underground slave-quarters or *ergastula* and the Celtic village community with its tribal ownership of the land, as I described in another book (*The English Countryman*). There is little evidence of Christianity permeating the Roman legionaries,[1] though of Mithraism plenty, partly because the early Church discouraged military service among its converts. Since the British Church was pure Celtic, it is clear that the same phenomenon appears in Goidelic, Brythonic and Belgic England as appeared in Judæa, namely a native, organic movement of freedom and light manifested from below confronting the static power of government above. What the relations of this movement were to the Celtic princes, of whom Gildas drew an unsavoury picture, or to the Roman authority nobody knows. What we do know is that the converted Arthurian court was the birth-place of Far Western chivalry and that St Patrick (432-61), before he was carried off to Ireland in a Gaelic raid up the Bristol Channel to herd pigs on Mount Miss, was the son of a harassed Romano-Celtic official, in the traditional home of King Arthur within the Severn borderland.

When St Patrick escaped from Ireland into Provence, he came into intimate contact along the Mediterranean coast with a chain of island or rather islet communities which St Ambrose compared with a necklace of pearls cast upon the waves, the like of which the world had never seen before nor has done since. Even the Bronze

---

[1] There was however a small basilican church within the walls of Silchester, or Calleva Atrebatum—likewise an amphitheatre for wild beast shows.

Age settlements on Dartmoor, on the Isle of Man and the Orkneys were less cut off from intercourse with the world's traffic than were monastic Calvaria, Gorgona, Palmaria, Gallinaria and Patrick's own Lerinus (Lérins) in the Tyrrhenian Sea, the abbott of which was a British monk, Faustus. The West had become a constellation of refugees from the universal pagan city-state into the bosom of wild nature. The monastic cells of Skellig Michael, the lump of crag off the coast of Kerry, were built on a platform 600 feet above the sea—five small beehive huts and two minute oratories, dry-walled and fenced within a wall whose outer face was flush with the precipice that walls the sea. A ladder of rude steps, hewn probably in the 6th century, leads a boating party up to this nick in the rock-cone, and here the brethren lived like a herd of goats.

The wildest isles round the wild Irish coast, the Blaskets, Inishmurray, the Arans, Clare and others, were alike populated by these auk-men, and the sound of their plain-chant must have often accompanied the hoarse primordial roar of the massed guillemots, itself responding to the more measured beat of the ocean breakers and the booming of the wind. In that primal scene the ear would have often caught a graded series of variations upon a single theme of elemental majesty, the tumult of the wind and the sea translated into the growling thunder of the white-breasted bird-ranks, and that in its turn transfigured into the harmonious Magnificat of the monkish antiphony. For these sainted sea-dogs were a bardic company. I have stroked an eider-duck on its pillow-nest among the thrift in the little sea-garden of St Cuthbert's Monastery on the Farnes, its downiest home among the elements, and in the act repeated what St Cuthbert doubtless did every summer day as due part of his matins.

The islets between and the rocky promontories on

35

the coasts of South Wales and Brittany became centres of learning and light, and St Illtyd on Caldey Island, St Cadoc of Llancarvon, St Samson, St Gildas and St David communicated with St Brendan of Clonfert, St Columba of Derny and Iona, St Ciaran of Clonmacnoise and St Finnian of Clonard. Beside St David's Cathedral, built on the foundation of a minute monastery, are three chapels by the sea and a fourth in Porth Stinian Bay, while David himself lived as a hermit on Ramsay Isle across the sound. Here on the moors, scarred by outcrop, where the buzzards perch or mew in the salt air, occurs one of these chapels side by side with a holy well and the remains of a stone circle. The story is plain : the sanctuaries of the older faiths in these lonely lands were reconsecrated to a life of contemplation and prayer, and the quarry-stone hauled by heathen hands was fitted into the chapel-walls of the new Faith. The native cultural tradition blended with the sympathetic Christian influences to produce a vernacular literature that was organic to the bone. Or, as Christopher Dawson has put it in *The Making of Europe :*

> "Thus there was no sudden break between the old barbaric tradition and that of the Church, such as occurred elsewhere, and a unique fusion took place between the Church and the Celtic tribal society entirely unlike anything else in Western Europe."

A new revelation of life but a continuity unbroken. Such is the inner meaning of the British Church.

> "They rear'd their lodges in the wilderness,
> Or built them cells beside the shadowy sea,
> And there they dwelt with angels, like a dream.
> So they unroll'd the Volume of the Book
> And fill'd the fields of the Evangelist
> With thoughts as sweet as flowers."

So Hawker of Morwenstow, whose Egeria was St

Morwenna of his native Duchy and who was himself a throw-back to the primitive Church.

This topographical pointer also guided St Patrick in his mission to the Isle of Saints, whither Pelagius had preceded him. St Patrick had actually more Roman associations than any of the long line of Far Western gospellers that followed him and built up an independent Western Christendom whose Eastern affinities were with the Greek rather than with the Roman. Perhaps that is one reason why he aimed his holy darts at the Celtic aristocracy of Ireland through which he obtained grants of land for his churches and monasteries rather than moved among and lit up the commoners, and conducted a series of thaumaturgic duels with the Druidic magicians. Yet he followed a deeper tradition when he spent forty days on the summit of Croagh Patrick, the sacred mount that had been the heathen high place. It is possible in a famous incident to catch a gleam of the new philosophy of heaven and earth in interdependence and interaction, formulated by a culture in such vital contact with the ancient nature-worship, by deliberate choice breaking completely with the city-state and making its homes in the wildest of wild places. This incident was the conversion in Connaught of the daughters of Loegaire, the High King of Tara, Ethne the Fair and Fedelm the Red. When they questioned him as to who the new God was and where he dwelt, Patrick replied :

"Our God is the God of all men, the God of heaven and earth, of sea and river, of sun and moon and stars, of the lofty mountain and the lowly valleys, the God above heaven and in heaven and under heaven ; he has his dwelling round heaven and earth and sea and all that in them is. He inspires all, he quickens all, he dominates all, he sustains all. He lights the light of the sun ; he furnishes the light of the light ; he has made springs in the dry land and has set stars to minister to the greater lights."

It is possible to see in this psalmic utterance more than the feelings made articulate of the solitaries and little clusters of cenobites and *familiæ* when confronted with light and space and wave and rock. It is a prevision, even a paraphrase, of Emily Brontë's :

" With wide-embracing love
Thy Spirit animates eternal years,
    Pervades and broods above,
Changes, sustains, dissolves, creates and rears."

II. The Interplay of Nature, Art and Religion.
Gougaud, in his *Christianity in Celtic Lands*, wrote :

"Let us draw attention to another feature of Celtic hagiography, to wit, the large space allotted in it to scenes of nature, familiar or picturesque, and to animals which are represented as at the Saint's beck and call."

Chevalier remarked upon the same :

"Celtic Christianity . . . is animated throughout by the love of nature and of native country, by a winning familiarity with our 'unknown brothers,' animals or angels, and by a passion for spirituality."

Helen Waddell, whose exquisite translations from the *Vitæ Sanctorum Hiberniæ* and other sources have ennobled 20th century literature, has stirred in us a wonder equally at the fey and primitive *naïveté* of these tales of communication between man and beast as at the profundity of what she calls their *pietas*.

St Kevin would not move his outstretched hand in prayer until a blackbird that had nested on his palm had hatched her young, and would not have the mountains about Glendalough levelled to make good pasture for the monks so as not to upset the natural ecology between the mountain fauna and their habitat. The *Vita Columbani* relates that, when St Columban walked through the forest, the birds in flocks would follow him from tree to tree, joyfully twittering, and the squirrels "would frisk along and gambol in great delight, like puppies fawning on their masters." St Columba, of the proud and passionate blood of the Celtic princes who converted the Picts by sheer audacity and high temper, is reported by Adamnan, his biographer (690), as nursing a crane on migration for three days and as being so beloved by his dairy horse that, when he knew he was to die, it shed tears on his breast.

A number of these tales must have come as near truth as may, since it is to be remembered that a hawk alighted on the muzzle of Darwin's gun when he landed on the Galápagos. Our estrangement from the creatures is mainly man-made. And it is noticeable that even the more fabulous stories never anthropomorphize their animals nor attempt to make them other than creaturely after their kind. A dragon appears among the eremites of the Eastern desert, but the naturalist has no quarrel with the familiars of St Ciaran, St Cuthbert and St Aidan. In their familiarity with sainthood they do not become outcasts from their own kingdom ; every beast and bird remains *sui generis*. The moral of every tale is the absence of fear on the part of the beast, of pursuit on the part of the man, and from mutual tolerance to amity is but a step. The beasts under the saintly spell were not denatured ; there is nothing Æsopian about them. Perhaps, too, the occultism of the Celt had a hand in it. What does emerge from this bestiary-hagiography in which man appears as the gentle paragon of animals is a symbolic drama of man as part of nature and man as child of God.

The records of the British Church disclose two interwoven strands of attachment to nature. The first is a unique passion for the wild and the elemental as though to break through the crust of artificial convention down to the very roots of sheer being and through the primal earth-life to strain towards the Divine Craftsman who said, "Before Abraham was, I am." It is a kind of expeditionary search to find not El Dorado but the Lost Paradise, when nature was virgin and unblemished, fresh from the celestial workshop. "Paradise," wrote Berdyaev in the *Destiny of Man*:

> "exists not merely in men's memories, dreams and creative imagination. It is promised in the beauty of nature, in the sunlight, the shining stars, the blue sky, the virgin snow of the mountain peaks, the seas and the rivers, the forests and cornfields, the precious stones and flowers and the splendour of the animal world. My salvation is bound up with that, not only of other men, but also of animals, plants, minerals, of every blade of grass—all must be transfigured and brought into the Kingdom of God."

The resemblance between this passage of a modern religious philosopher and that of St Patrick's words to the daughters of Loegaire needs no emphasis. Again :

> "Love for the creature in general, for animals, plants, minerals, for the earth and the stars, has not been at all developed in Christian ethics . . . It has not worked out an ethics of love for the world, for all created things and all living beings."

If the British Church had survived, it is possible that the fissure between Christianity and nature, widening through the centuries, would not have cracked the unity of Western man's attitude to the Universe. It was the pantheist like W. H. Hudson, the great primitive, who delivered the modern praise of creation, not the Christian. It was the diarist, Dorothy Wordsworth, who wrote of "the unworldliness of nature" and Loch Etive as "among the grandest works of God," who came nearer to the spirit of these primitive pioneers than do any of the modern Churches, whose evolution has been heavier in loss than in gain.

Secondly, the British Church was a flowering from the native stem of the Celtic culture ; though it extended its sprays over Western Europe, its roots were in its own soil as the regional Church of the Far West. Not a few of the Abbots and the *Peregrini* were themselves of royal or noble houses, Columba, Morban, a king's brother, and Cronan of the Glen, the piper saint. As I have said, the bardic tradition of the Celts was maintained by the brethren and the bardic schools were reorganized by Columba. It is interesting that St Aldhelm, the patron saint of Dorset, who danced and sang his own melodies in the streets of Sherborne for the joy of the gospel, received his early education at Malmesbury at the hands of St Maelduth, its founder. Many lives of the Irish saints were actually written at Glastonbury. St Motacilla, the patroness of the hunted hare, was a Welsh princess. She seems own sister to Hawker of Morwenstow's St Clare in the spirit—St Morwenna. The nonnaturalistic geometric art of the Celts with its zoomorphic decoration received an immense stimulus from the British Church with its key, diaper, interlacing and spiral patterns. Being on sympathetic terms with the natural kingdom did not mean drawing or carving it from nature. The famous font at Deerhurst-on-Severn is much more Hiburnian than Saxon, and the High Crosses of Ireland owe their decorative motives to the Celtic genius and Celtic forms of design. For the same reason this native bent for intricate ornament, fantastic invention and a stylized fauna and flora was amateurish with the human figure even at the height of its Christian Renaissance. Even where Hellenic and Syriac influences crept in upon this native art, they enriched its resources without distracting its inspiration.

41

The Tree of Life

III. The Native Independence of the Western Church.

The remarkable independence of the British Church not only of the Roman deified state but of Roman ecclesiasticism was the supreme expression of its native and regional origins, background, environment. Not, of course, that the British Church was spontaneously generated. We know that it came from Palestine, and it is likely that it came *via* Rome. It was springing up when most of Britain was part of the Roman Empire. Of this the basilican church at Silchester is plain proof, and Professor Chadwick's opinion is that there was widespread continuity in the uses of churches and church sites from the Roman to the English period. It is also certain that intercourse between the Church in Britain and on the Continent was maintained after the departure of the legions. The date used by the British for keeping Easter when Augustine landed was the date adopted by Rome about 70 years earlier. Thus there was no entirely separate British Church : what we can say is that it diverged from the main phylum and took on a native character peculiar to itself alone. It was in no sense a breaking-away from Rome, like the Reformation.

What we can also say is that the seeds sown by the flying Dove of the Holy Spirit became the mustard tree of the Far West. There was in no sense a conscious hostility to the Roman communion. Adamnan's Life of Columban, for instance, does not argue against Rome : it does not mention Rome, and the controversial difference with Rome over the tonsure and the date of Easter (which seems trivial enough to us) never became acute until just before the Synod of Whitby in 664. Augustine, whose prize was Kent only, made several attempts to bring the recalcitrant and indigenous Church to book, but, avoiding logomachy, it went serenely on, netting its great draughts of converts, colonizing wastes, permeating courts, missionizing far horizons and pursuing its own distinctive forms of growth without either resisting or yielding to the call of discipline. Dinoot, Abbot of Bangor, wrote to Augustine :

> "I am willing to show the Pope of Rome the affection and charity which I ought to feel for every Christian ; more I do not owe to him whom you call the Pope and who wrongfully claims to be the father of fathers."

This home-made though still universal Church had its own hagiography and acknowledged Christ, not the Pope, as its supreme head. There was no inequality between men and women, and confession was voluntary. Columban indeed, the very prince of the *Peregrini*, founded his clusters of cells in the heart of the Carolingian Empire and at Bobbio as far as the Apennines. They went everywhere, scattering blessings, inducing peace, taming barbarians and planting new monasteries but without ever compromising or diluting their Western culture and their Western freedom. No matter how far the pilgrims travelled, they took their wild homes with them, just as the Polynesian voyagers more literally carried their own soils in their colonization of the Pacific Isles. So our pacific islanders carried their Celticism, culture, worship, ethos and all. Even to the court of Charlemagne the wind and the sea went with them. An Irish scribe in the monastery of St Gall in Switzerland wrote this madrigal translated by Kuno Meyer (*Ancient Irish Poetry*) :

> "A hedge of trees surrounds me,
> A blackbird's lay sings to me ;
>   Above my linèd booklet
> The trilling birds chant to me.
>
> In a grey mantle from the top of bushes
>   The cuckoo sings :
> Verily—may the Lord shield me !—
> Well do I write under the greenwood."

This was our pre-Saxon, vernacular Church whom their very competitors, as Toynbee has pointed out, who robbed them of their birthright of independence, enlisted in the fertilization of the Carolingian Renaissance.

The effect of this was, as Toynbee says, in his *Study of History*, to "encourage a libertarian genius" which actually was the cause of their defeat when they did come into conflict with the authority of Rome. One of their great scholars, Johannes Scotus Erigena, "declared for reason against authority and put philosophy on an equal footing with theology." Pelagius, a heretic of the Roman, was a member of the British Church, which was only very lightly episcopal and so disciplinary. Pelagius is not perhaps a feather in the cap of any Church, but his membership of our primitive Church is a good example of its tolerance and intellectual liberty. Even its Holy Mother was St Bridget rather than St Mary.

In a sombre world which, as our own does, blindly gropes after a machinery of organization, for external in place of self-government, for orders rather than order to subdue if not to resolve its own self-created chaos, the free spirit and organic self-help of the British Church were indeed too much in advance of their time. The clash between freedom and authority, between, it might be said, the country and the town, was drawn to a point of pregnant and dramatic intensity when Rome met Lindisfarne at the court of Oswy of Northumbria at Whitby. The King gave his adherence to Wulfrid, the plaintiff for Peter, lest, as he said, "when I come to the gates of the Kingdom of Heaven, there should be none to open to me, he being my adversary who is proved to have the keys." Colman, the British champion, had nothing to say ; for him, as for Hamlet, "the rest is silence." The British Church went no further than that closed door. It retired upon itself as many a life-bringer has done since, and thenceforward it shrank in influence and perhaps in dynamic power until the barbarian hurricane of the Northmen overwhelmed it. It does not speak too well for Bede, the representative of the new Anglo-Roman Church but otherwise a panegyrist of Celtic sainthood, that, when the monks of Bangor were massacred by King Ethelfrid of Northumbria's Saxons, he as good as said that it served them right.

There can be no doubt that its mixed racial humus has been mainly responsible for the particular virtue of historic England. Both Collingwood (*Roman Briton*) and Thurlow Leeds (*The Archæology of the Anglo-Saxon Settlements*) are agreed that the origins and inspiration of the beautiful Anglican art are to be sought out of the more ancient and conquered culture. In the fabric of the English tradition we may detect a bright thread that wanders seemingly at its own sweet will from one part of the design to another, touching them all with flame. It is hardly too much to say that the first hand that stitched in this free colour when the frame was making was that of the British Church. In Ireland, it was too early torn out.

No reader of the annals of this primitive Church can think of it as other than one of the supreme miracles of history. It is stuffed with paradox, as itself was for six centuries the leaven to the dough of average humanity. The paradox of extreme mobility with fixity in inaccessible places, of asceticism with freedom of thought, of culture, learning and art with the roughest living in the rudest of homes, of studiousness and hardiness, of the highest spirituality in the humblest of dwellings, of wisdom and childlikeness, of wholeness and multiplicity of living with "Seek ye first the Kingdom of Heaven." The wondering explorer who travels in those ancient footsteps to rocky islets over tussocky saltings, through what Dorothy Wordsworth called "moorish" wildernesses, will be confronted with another paradox, equally potent.

He will ask himself in these solitudes not only how these fellow-residents of buzzards and guillemots came to conquer with their glad tidings a Western world almost as dark with strife and confusion as our own, but how in such places did they manage to live at all? The monastic and especially the modern literature whose subject is the heroic humility of these wild monks is exasperatingly reticent upon this very pertinent and vital issue. It occurs to hardly any of these writers to enquire how, if manna was not dropped upon these remote settlements from the storm-clouds and if ravens companioned but did not actually feed them like Elijah, how, especially in the larger colonies, they supported themselves. By collecting gulls' eggs, by frying seaweed, by plucking whortleberries and wild strawberries?

IV. The Husbandry of the Wilds.

The consequence is that what scraps and leavings of information are to be picked out are casual and in parenthesis. And the question is the more wonder-making when it is considered that the sea-journeys of these intrepid monk-mariners over the Atlantic appear to have been in coracles of wicker and hide, so that the legendary as well as heavenly light that plays upon St Brendan, who founded Clonfert and yet was a reborn pagan Bran who voyaged towards the land of the sunset, the Tir Na Nog, the Isles of the Blest, is less miraculous than the boat he sailed in. It is evident that the monkish Thoreaus and Alastors could not have depended upon imported food-supplies; their communities must have been self-sufficient. What we do learn is that Columba's monastery on Iona was surrounded by a rampart or *cashel* of timber and that outside it was a barn, a byre, a kiln for drying corn, a mill, a fish-pond, pasture and fields in tillage. The cultivators were the working brethren, like the Cistercian *conversi*, who combined the seasonal round of husbandry with dairying, metal-work, building, illuminating and vellum-painting. On the day of his death in 597, he went to the barn and blest the labour of the brethren, he blest the white dairy-horse that placed its head on his breast and then went to his cell to write his last words : "They that serve the Lord shall not want any good thing." Thus religion, learning, the arts and crafts, agriculture and the contemplation of wild nature as the manifestation of God, were integrated as aspects of one whole.

Other agrarian detail is of the scantiest. We learn that many of the monasteries were centres of gardening and orcharding—would that we knew what flowers and what fruit ! When Honoratus first landed on Lerinus, where St Patrick received his education between his escape from and his mission to Ireland, he found it a "snake-infested" waste. His reclamation work consisted in the building of cells, the digging of wells, the sowing of corn and the planting of vines. St Cuthbert of Melrose, before he became an itinerant and had become a solitary on the Farnes, was a shepherd on the Lammermoors. Of the 950 monks under St Kentigern at St Asaph, 300 of them were husbandmen, but all the brethren had workshops. The *Vita Davidis* relates that in some of the British monasteries the labour of the fields was conducted without any animals of transport or burden at all, "every one being his own ox and his own horse." The monks fed the flocks, gathered the harvest, threshed the corn with rude flails and ground it on hand-querns. They grew their own vegetables, baked their own bread, drank milk and whey, were fish- and egg-eaters (whether from wild or domestic fowl is not stated) and served venison and pork to their guests. The farms appear to have been held communally as on Iona. There is no doubt that these monkish settlements accomplished a work of reclamation not less arduous if less renowned than that of the Cistercians in Yorkshire, not only in wild places but, as Christopher Dawson points out, among lands made derelict by military invasion.

Side by side with this post-paradisal Adamite agriculture, the most elaborate and delicate craftsmanship was practised in vellum-painting, illumination and lettering, in carving and goldsmith work. In the monastic schools and the universities at Clonfert, Clonmacnoise, Moville, Bangor and elsewhere, history, biography, grammar, the classics, poetry, letters and even archæology were taught *in conjunction* with a great variety of handicrafts in metal, wood, leather and bronze. To what a pitch of finished complexity the decorative work on the manuscripts reached may be gathered from the fact that in a space of three-quarters of by half an inch 158 interlacements have been counted without a single false line. From these schools and universities sallied forth the Odyssean *peregrini* and the *episcopi vagantes* as far as Iceland and perhaps America, often in bands of twelve with a leader to convert, to soften, to humanize and to educate a savage and turbulent world. But where they started from is best described in a piece from the Irish Triads of the 9th century and quoted by Eileen Power :

> "Three slender things that best support the world : the slender stream of milk from the cow's dug into the pail ; the slender blade of green corn upon the ground ; the slender thread over the hand of a skilled woman. Three sounds of increase : the lowing of a cow in milk ; the din of a smithy ; the swish of a plough."

This colossal achievement in the colonization of the wilds, as outstanding, if not at all celebrated, as the cultural and religious conquests, could never have been accomplished if the monkish settlers had not been country-

men themselves. They were thus in a peculiar relation
to the native peasantry enjoyed by no other missionary
movement in the world's history. St Walaric, who
founded St Valéry-sur-Somme, was himself a peasant,
while St Theodulph, the Abbot of St Thierry, was a
husbandman of such indefatigable personal labour that
at his death the peasants hung up his plough as a
memorial in the Church, while the holy tree that sprang
from the oxgoad he had plunged into the soil was
honoured by them as the Wiltshire villagers honoured
Hudson's "Old Thorn." Not only did these Christian
heroes understand the peasant culture, not only did they
practise the peasant husbandry and the peasant crafts,
not only did they transform without trampling under-
foot peasant custom and belief—the tumulus crowned
by the chapel, the menhir carved into the high cross,
the sacred reconsecrated into the holy well—but in so
acting they were translating into a new symbolic and
realistic language of life for the West to read the example
of their own Master in Galilee. They came to refashion,
to purify, to garden *what was already there*, not to displace
it with something else. This quintessential point is
what has been missed by the modern commentators
on the lives of the primitive saints of the West. Christopher Dawson, after mentioning with approval Maurice
Barrès's urban and myopic judgment about "the sinister
powers of the old nature religion still latent in the
European countryside," cancels it a few lines later by:

> "Nevertheless, it is remarkable that it is just in those
> regions where the external survivals of pagan customs
> are most noticeable, as in Brittany and the Tirol, that
> the Christian ethos has affected the life of the peasant
> most deeply."

This without doubt was the work of the British Church.
Demonic Druidism, like its predecessor, the megalithic

cult of the dead, was a kingly and aristocratic privilege, not a peasant religion.

The hackneyed "faith can move mountains" was more than fulfilled in its history, since it moved something more obdurate than any mountain, the mind of man. It is beside this mountainous faith in Christ as not only the Redeemer of the world but with God as its Creator, faith in the rural Christ and its significations, that Toynbee's word in the *Study of History* should be juxtaposed:

> "The extinction of faith is being recognized as the supreme danger to the spiritual health and even to the material existence of the Western body social—a deadlier danger by far than any of our hotly canvassed and loudly advertised political and economic maladies. To refill the spiritual vacuum . . . is the most formidable and the most urgent of all problems that are remorselessly crowding upon the present generation."

It was a faith based on such foundations and such elementals as is summed up in its earthly context by these words of H. D. C. Pepler in the *Weekly Review* of July 23, 1942:

> "I would go back to the grain and the furrow, the horse and the plough, the millstone and the fishing boat, the family and the home where things and people are made, knowing perfectly well that if these primaries are well done, all other matters will fall into their right places."

Out of beginnings even simpler and more primary than horse and plough, out of the very heart of wild nature sprang a clothed and sacred Minerva, unified in every part, whose wisdom was of God's presence and work in nature and in man. The primitive British Church expressed both in their homely lives and their apostolic journeys, both in their works and their habita-

50

tions, something more than beliefs it is customary to call Christian. This something more was a sanctification of the entire world of nature, and if the form it took appears to us to belong rather to the childhood than the adulthood of man, the conception itself is surely as indispensable for maturity as for youth, for ends as for beginnings.

CHAPTER FOUR

THE MIDDLE AGES AND THE NATURAL LAW.

I. The Rise and Fall of the Cistercians.

THE Cistercian Order was the most direct legatee of the British Church. Both professed and practised a husbandry in which farming was part of religion, and religion was in daily contact with nature. I have already given a brief account of the creative growth and discreditable decay of the Cistercians in my *English Countryman*. But I must here supplement that spare pen-portrait by illustrating their break with the unity of man's religious attitude to nature and consider as parallel to it a further estrangement which the body of religious thought suffered during the Middle Ages.

For two reasons the Cistercians are one of the nodal points in this narrative. First, they were the heirs of the British Church in a more direct line than were the other religious Orders of the Middle Ages. Secondly, Stephen Harding's logos by which their activities were governed—to labour is to pray—is the secret of craftsmanship which is organically related to nature on the one hand and to religion on the other. The craftsman's work, whose by-product is the instinctive beauty derived from nature, is at the same time worship as a microcosm of the Creation. This double relation was clearly acknowledged first by the British Church and then by the Cistercians.

The whole principle of Cistercian agriculture was the reclamation and colonization of waste places. This was the root of what Maitland called "the extraordinary

52

benefit they conferred upon mankind," as craftsmen-cultivators, as benevolent landlords and as intelligent farmers. The history of their early wanderings and privations, outlined in Dugdale's *Monasticon*, reveals that the choice of wild places was as deliberate as though less uncompromising than that of the British evangelists. There they drained marshes, made roads, embanked rivers, bridged them, planted woodlands, set up mills, fisheries and salt-works, quarried their own stone and built their early churches with their own hands. In their able and diligent charge craftsmanship assumed its proper planetary position in the solar system of agriculture. The Cistercian idea of wholeness as inseparable from holiness faithfully translated into action the recognition of Christ both as transcendental Godhead and the Peasant-Craftsman on earth who expressed a cosmic wisdom in the terms of peasant speech.

The Cistercian community fulfilled the richest potentialities of peasant economy, self-sufficient in every age and in all countries where not crippled or abolished by urban civilization. The monks rose at 2 a.m. from their straw-beds and, after prayer and meditation until daylight, went out into the fields, abbot and all, wearing the cheapest undyed frieze of the country. Each monk had one pound of rye bread and two dishes of vegetables for his two meals a day. They brewed beer and made home-wines ; they worked the iron and lead which they used in their churches ; they stocked the uplands with sheep, spun wool and built their own warehouses for it ; they bred horses and stock for use on the farms and were the great bee-masters of the Middle Ages. The abbey cellarer's function in the fields exactly corresponded with that of the village reeve, while their own *conversi* or lay-workers corresponded with the freer villeins of the more responsible and enlightened manorial estates. The Lady Poverty reigned in equal state on the abbey estates as the Virgin, with patience, frugality and above all charity as her attendants. That poverty was turned into plenty when the abbeys entertained, and their regional unity stood in dramatic contrast with our modern separatism when Fountains or Byland or Jervaulx or Tintern was not only a guest-house but an almshouse, a hospital and an agricultural college as well. A Cistercian manor was a "felde ful of folke," and the workers in it were the children of St Theodulph the Ploughman.

A step from the 13th to the 14th century and all is changed, and that success which has been the modern criterion of worth was first the corruption and then the undoing of the Cistercian Brotherhood. Lucifer the light-bringer was transformed into Lucifer the fallen angel. An austere simplicity had reared abbeys and churches whose grandeur and spirituality depended upon architectural lines that eschewed because they had no need of ornament. It became warped and twisted into the complexity which attends the acquisition of riches. The Cistercian monks acquired land at such a prodigious speed that the husbandmen who had brooded over and tended their smaller properties with the yeoman's personal devotion became metamorphosed into absentee landlords. This functionless estate-holding drew them in its turn into endless litigation. They who had planted their first standards in the wild by building granges and cloisters of mud, chapels of wood, and had considered manual labour as an equal oblation to God with prayer, waxed fat and lazy by the reception of mere rents. They derived an unearned income by the mere possession of those sheep of which they had been the greatest of all flockmasters and experimental breeders. In the 13th century, they had by personal superintendence reared the Lion breed of Cotswolds that made the fortune of 14th century England and of which but one small

54

flock now remains in all the world ; in the 14th, they drew the revenues which their estate-managers collected for them and quarrelled, these once men of peace and poverty, so violently over them with other country magnates that they hired mercenaries to sabotage decisions that went against them.

The producers of plenty out of barren places became traders and dealers in wool. Their monasteries became corporations. The keepers of the Rule who had worked side by side with the peasants shepherding the abbey flocks, setting plough, drying barley in the malt-house and grafting Warden pears from Burgundy in Yorkshire orchards, now thought of nothing but laying field to field, flock to flock, house to house and chattel to chattel. Their mixed craftsmanship and mixed agriculture, demonstrated by the hardly credible variety of their occupations both on and by the land, were telescoped into multiplying sheep on ranches. These had reverted to the wilds from which they had been reclaimed so that Sir Thomas More, the champion who lost his head for their religion, said of them : "They have no grounds for tillage, they enclose all into pastures." Their sheep "did consume, destroye and devoure whole fieldes, houses and cities" ; the very church was degraded into a sheep-house, while "the pryse of wolle be so rysen that poor folkes . . . be nowe hable to buy none at all." In all history there is no tragedy more deep-seated, no irony more acute and no retribution more melancholy and well-deserved than the *corruptio optimi pessima* of the Cistercians. When one more covetous and power-intoxicated than themselves stretched out a mailed fist with an itching palm for their wealth in sheep and horses, it seemed to be the very hand of justice. Lilies that fester smell far worse than weeds.

II. *The Religious Change towards Nature.*

As a religious culture the entire Middle Ages are properly regarded as remarkably uniform both in length and in depth, like, for all its complex and multiform elements, one of their own cathedrals. Nevertheless, a division within the unity can be detected, and the Cistercian self-contradiction partly reveals what it was. In the very broadest sense, it was a developing compromise rather than a revolutionary break with the ideal of primitive Christianity, as exemplified by the early Church and formulated by the life of Christ. It may be summed up, also in the most general terms, as a gradual change-over from a sense of responsibility to a sense of power, and this is reflected by a corresponding change in philosophic concept. Dr G. G. Coulton has written many books on mediæval social history, one of the main objects of which appears to be the denigration and debunking of the religious Orders. When, therefore, their good works do find a place in his scholarly records, in, for instance, *The Mediæval Village*, his testimony, based on exhaustive knowledge, is of the highest value. In the issue of the relation between monk and peasant, he quotes the Cluniac Peter the Venerable in answer to St Bernard, that, whereas lay lords treated their serfs without justice or mercy,

> "yet monks, although they own serfs, own them differently. For they use the due and lawful services of these people only for their own livelihood, vex them with no exaction, lay no unbearable burdens upon them, and, if they see them in want, even support them from their own possessions. They treat their own bondmen and bondwomen not as bondmen and bondwomen but as brothers and sisters."

I recently discovered from the local records that, when the village of Yarnton (Oxon) passed into the charge of the Cistercian Abbey of Rewley, the villagers were freed from all dues, fines, inquisitions and forced services, while the Rogation ceremony there of blessing the fields (pagan in origin) survived, before a bypass were driven through the lot-meadows, in a garland of grasses woven for the altar. It may be taken, then, that, in the golden age of monachism, the relation of monk to peasant was one, commonly speaking, of responsibility. It acknowledged the Fatherhood of God over both in a common service of the earth. It nourished the husbandman and the craftsman who wrought alike in the materials of nature.

This impression is reinforced by the attitude of the early Latin Church towards nature. E. I. Watkin, in *Catholic Art and Culture*, points out that the emblem principally represented in the Catacombs was not the crucified Christ but the Good Shepherd, a happy, peaceful figure who resembled Hermes or Orpheus. So in the vision of St Satyrus, heaven was "a garden bearing rose trees and all kinds of flowers." Boniface was a good backwoodsman, and Clement of Alexandria wrote : "As beauty, so also the flower delights when looked at ; and it is meet to glorify the Creator by the enjoyment of the sight of beautiful objects." Basil the Great, who spoke of the stars as the undying flowers of the sky ; St Hilary, who wrote a Morning Hymn of the sun ; St Chrysostom, to whom as to W. H. Hudson the work of art was not to be compared with the work of nature, these and others were Christian contemplatives who found in solitude and nature the "sweetest of all fruits, tranquillity." Gregory Nazianzen wrote :

> "I used to walk by myself about sunset and used to spend my time by the sea-shore ; for I was accustomed to make use of this recreation to refresh myself, and to shake off some of my ordinary troubles."

This is paralleled by St Bernard of Clairvaux's description

of the sick man (quoted by Robert Burton) who sits upon a green bank and

> "feeds his eyes with variety of objects, herbs, trees, to comfort his misery ; he receives many delightsome smells, and fills his ears with the sweet and various harmony of birds : Good God, saith he, what a company of pleasures hast Thou made for man !"

The likeness of this apostrophe to Izaak Walton's on the nightingale—"Lord, what music . . . "—is striking.

It cannot be claimed that a silver anthology of such sayings can compare with the passion for wild nature which runs like a flame through the whole history of the British Church. The difference, of course, was partly environmental, the Mediterranean being a region of city-states, but it was also racial and temperamental. The only figure in the Roman Church who can be so compared is St Francis, whose *Fioretti* exhibit an imaginative and acutely sensitive animism, not different *in kind* from that of primitive man. St Francis, who was careful not brusquely to put out a candle flame, who spoke of water as his sister and handled stones reverently in building a wall, had a decided kinship of spirit with the elementalism of the Celtic saints. It is at once moral and deeper than moral. But it is not remote from the craftsman's and artist's handling of natural materials *as though* a spirit abode in each one, different each according to its nature, to be persuaded and caressed, not coerced, into doing its office in the service of man. W. H. Hudson's frequent outbursts of animism and Shakespeare's treatment of Ariel have the same affinity with Franciscan, Celtic and primitive animism. In the Celtic saints, this animism is transfigured, not repudiated.

III. The Peasantry and Power-Politics.

St Francis's animism was fused with his faithful self-dedication to the Lady Poverty and his supreme personal devotion to his Master. It could not, therefore, survive in its Christian form and in lesser beings with the change in the economic position of the abbeys and monasteries and the new post-Hildebrandine power-politics in the Papacy. Let me take these changes one by one. Perhaps a milestone in the deviation of the first from the practice of primitive Christianity is simply when the monks ceased to labour with their hands. As early as 1310, Henry, the Abbot of Cluny, passed a statute that it was "unbecoming for God's soldiers to be entangled in worldly business," and forbidding "any of our Order should keep hawks, falcons or other birds of chase or hunting dogs," exempting, however, those in the monasteries who had "the right, custom and usage of hunting." Much later, both Langland in *Piers Plowman* and Gower, Chaucer's contemporary, drew satiric pictures of the hunting monk, not dissimilar from Sydney Smith's of the hunting parson or "squarson" in the 17th century. When monks became notorious for keeping hunting stables, it is clear that we are a long way from the Cistercian labour of the fields.

It is equally clear that when they became rich and powerful enough to be absentee landlords, they lost touch with the life of the peasant. In spite of Dr Coulton's perseverance in whittling down the credit of the monasteries, there can be no real doubt that they made on the whole better landlords than the lay lords. But the more farms and estates they controlled, the less personal control over and so responsibility for their administration. The middleman began to set the pace, not the monk. And this loosening of the ties of trusteeship actually corresponded with a marked improvement, in England at any rate, in the conditions of the peasantry itself. That is to say, the peasants bought themselves out of their forced services on the monastic estates, not by the goodwill of the clerical landlords, but simply because it became more profitable for the clerical estate to become a rent-receiver. The manumission of the bondman was achieved by his own co-operative enterprise and determination. That this was so is sufficiently attested by the Peasants' Revolt of 1381, when a split between the higher and lower clergy became manifest in the support of the peasants by John Ball and his kind against their own superiors. There is a deep historical significance in the primitive Christianity not only preached by John Ball but common to the whole body of the peasantry in the revolt of the "great society" against both the great ecclesiastics and the great lords. This higher clergy had forfeited its inheritance in the mission of the Galilean peasant, as a century and a half later it was to forfeit the lands which had been the occasion of that spiritual loss. Chaucer's *povre Persoun* is represented as the true spiritual leader of the village community and so as the ambassador of his Master in Galilee.

> "A bettre preest I trowe that nowher seen ys,
> But Christes lore, and his Apostles twelve
> He taughte, but first he folwed it himselve."

The spiritual history of the Papacy ran more or less parallel with that of the Cistercians in England, both in date and in temper. It was never, of course, illiberal in its attitude towards the local self-government of the town-guilds and the village community as modern government has so pronouncedly been. Had it been so, local co-operation, small mastership and self-sufficiency both in trades and localities could never have flourished so superabundantly as they did. The Papacy's denunciation of usury and support of the principle of the Just Price, that keystone of the free-standing mediæval arch, were consistently maintained up to the end of the 13th century. Yet with the fall of the Hildebrandine

Church, a definite change can be detected, which Toynbee, in his *Study of History*, attributes to the devastation of the struggle between the Papacy and the Hohenstauffen Empire. In the 12th and 13th centuries (the papal claims being by exception high in the Pontificates of Innocent III (1198-1216) and Boniface VIII (1294-1303)), the Papacy was a spiritual authority, a *Respublica Christiana*, without territorial ambitions or attempting "to trespass upon the domain of the secular power." Valiant and faithful souls of almost infinite variety in talent and aptitude gathered to its service and it gave creative leadership to the inward and natural growth of Western civilization from its true basis in the soil and in the Incarnation. It recognized that all social institutions were, in Tawney's words (*The Acquisitive Society*) "an outward and imperfect expression of a supreme spiritual reality." If the Papacy made great deals with the financial houses and vested interests of Flanders, Rome and Florence at an early date, mediæval society as a whole favoured the traditional economic morality of Christendom that was solid with the small producer against the free play of capitalism and looked upon the owner as false to his privileges if he ceased to be the responsible trustee.

The failure of capitalism to corner the wool-trade in 15th century England has been vividly described by Eileen Power (*The Wool Trade in Mediæval England*). It is an eloquent example of the control of economic expediency by the moral authority. Up to the end of the 13th century, the Papacy was an active and generative force on behalf of the supreme idea that "God so loved the world that he gave his only-begotten son . . .," an idea of entrance into the world quite different from the Stoic philosopher's detachment from it, as has been well brought out by Toynbee. The concept of the material world as a temporal extension in time of eternal truth still governed the spiritual governor of the Western world.

The passing of the Hildebrandine Popes reversed, in Toynbee's words, the Papacy's alliance with spiritual freedom in its conflict with material force. Force was opposed by force and the papal crime was "felony against itself." In this suicidal policy, the vacant house was taken by the seventy-seven devils of the new secularism which in our own day has reached its final expression in the totalitarian State and the worship of the golden calf. Simony, financial exaction, territorialism, speculation and the replacement of the spiritual by the material sword, power-politics and the Great Schism to cap all, "these false prophets of an odious idolatry sat in Hildebrand's seat," and the tragedy of Periclean Athens was repeated. The grim causation from *koros* to *hubris* and from *hubris* to *ate* which Toynbee illustrates in the careers of civilization after civilization was set in motion. For man abhors a spiritual vacuum, and if the prodigal son deserts his home, he will eat husks with the swine. In Toynbee's striking parallel, if Gethsemane lost, Sparta was better than nothing. From the later Middle Ages to the present day the history of Western Europe has been that of the intensification of war, first religious and then economic wars, until the whole fabric has come to the point, unless some drastic rehabilitation takes place, of total collapse as the consequence of total war. Toynbee ends his survey of papal history with the question, "has Christianity still the power to release the soul of *Homo occidentalis* from the grip of a hideous and destructive paganism by offering a higher positive alternative?" The answer may be ventured—not until the mortal wound that severed the natural world from that of eternity has been healed.

IV. The Concept of the Natural Law.

This reflection brings me into direct contact with the mediæval concept of the natural law, which is remarkably unanimous 'throughout the Middle Ages. The Fathers and the early Christian writers preached a social doctrine as remote as it well could be from all modern forms of State autocracy. St Ambrose's doctrine of common property in land is St Chrysostom's "Let all of you sell all you have and bring it to a common fund." Gregory Nazianzen's common heritage of God's earth is on all fours with Ambrose's "The earth is all men's, not the property of the rich," Jerome's "all riches are born of iniquity and the spoliation of others," and Gregory the Great's "The land, the source of revenue, is the common property of all men, and for this reason its fruits are yielded for the common use of all." Basil's "If every man took but what sufficed for his own need, and left what is over for the needy, no one would be rich and no one poor" is to be equated with Augustine's "It is because of private possessions that lawsuits, hatreds, discords, wars among men, riots, civil dissensions, scandals, sins, iniquities and homicide arise." According to the teaching of the Fathers, not private property but its misuse transgresses the natural law which, as Chrysostom points out in his criticism of Plato, is less likely to be observed in the city than in the country : "His doctrine is only to be understood by the learned, but labourers, masons and sailors can see ours ; his plans are all city ones, ours do in deserts also."

The Pauline conception of the primal innocence (endorsed by the most recent anthropology) logically pronounced the equality of the "natural" man and that slavery is "contrary to nature" (Florentinus). It was, as R. W. and A. J. Carlyle categorically state in *Mediæval Political Theory in the West*) (Vol. V) reiterated by all the Fathers from St Irenæus in the 2nd century and

Augustine in the 5th to Gregory the Great in the 6th. When the rich man came to the rescue of the poor, his was an act of reparation and justice, not of charity. Government was necessary only because man had departed from God, and coercive government clean contrary to the Christian Faith. Paul's "ye are all in Jesus Christ" is the essence of the early Christian teaching. Private property was permissible because man had fallen from the state of primal innocence in the bosom of nature, but only as a stewardship and in trust (Basil). Thus, government, which is non-natural and so the result of sin, can only justify itself in so far as it controls the appetites let loose by the fall from nature and the divine grace. The Golden Age is recognized, indeed taken for granted, as a universal verity in which the divine order is indivisible from the natural order under the Fatherhood of God. Justice and equality are the birthright of *nature*. The same thought in a more comprehensive form appears six centuries later in Thomson's

> "Let us praise the impartiality of our Mother Nature, the most venerable, the ever young, the fountain of true democracy, the generous annunciator of true liberty and equality and fraternity; who bestoweth on all her children alike all things most necessary to true health and wealth, the sunshine, the air, the water, the fruits of the earth, and opens to rich and poor alike the golden doors of enfranchisement and initiation into the mysteries of heroism, purity, wisdom, beauty and infinite love."

But there is a difference : Christian theories of the natural law were based on the realism of the Incarnation ; this passage accepts and praises the gift without acknowledging the Giver.

This patristic doctrine was safely carried through, like the guarded Ark of the Covenant, up to the close of the 13th century.[1] Alexander of Hales (*ob.* 1245) : "Natural law ordains the equal freedom of all in the state of original nature ; but according to the state of fallen nature claims that subjection and lordship are necessary for the constraint of evil." St Bonaventure (1221-74) : "Freedom is in man by nature, but the power of lordship is destructive of freedom ; therefore lordship would seem not to be from nature." Again, law is not according to nature because "Do good to others" is a natural law. Rathenius, Bishop of Verona in the 10th century, said that all men were of one origin and one substance, all under one Father *in nature.* He is nobler who observes the law of nature than the prince who violates it by power. Even the feudal lawyers and jurists held that man's subjection to man was not natural but conventional. For them the natural law was "a body of principles apprehended by human reason as governing life and conduct, principles recognized as always just and good" (the Carlyles).

Of the mediæval civilian views Placentinus and Grotian declared nature to be equivalent to God who caused all, things to be brought forth. Natural was supreme law, "the principles by which the world is governed," and a rescript of the emperor contrary to it was invalid. Rufinus wrote that natural law has taught all animals and was implanted in man to make him moral. Hugolinus, Athenicus and Grotian identified the *jus naturale* with the *jus divinum*, while Stephen of Tournai maintained that the natural-divine law for men and animals was immutable. The Pope himself, according to Damasus, could not change it. No dispensation from the natural law was acceptable except as a choice between two evils. Where institutions conflicted with the *jus naturale*, it was the difference between primeval or natural and actual or conventional law. Christ said,

[1] *See* Bede Jarrett's *Social Theories of the Middle Ages* (1936).

"I am the truth," not "I am custom or constitution."
No man has the right to take more than he needs ; if
he does it is theft, a statement entirely harmonious with
that of the Decretal Law of Responsibility, that a man
can only be said to possess that of which he makes good
use. Bad use forfeits that possession.

The Carlyles have admirably summed up this tremendous testimony, accepted by so many ages and distributed
over so many countries, as

> "this majestic conception of law presented by civilians
> and canonists, referring not to mere will or power of
> community or ruler, but an attempt to translate into
> terms and adapt to the conditions of daily life those
> ultimate principles of equity and justice by which the
> whole universe was controlled and ordered."

It is plain that a mediæval thought thus orientated
could allow, to quote Tawney's words, "no division
between the inner life and the external order," and
could not do other than denounce usury or the misuse
of ownership as a violation of the natural law.

Whether or no it was justified by the facts of nature
is for later enquiry. But one has only to compare with
the *jus naturale* the idolatry of Humanity with a capital H
of the Positivists and latter-day humanists, the degenerate
pantheism of the Shavian life-forcers or the impersonal
cosmologies of modern fancy-religions or, worst of all,
the deified State, to perceive that they are as ephemeral
as though less to be regretted than Herrick's daffodils.
But the *lex suprema Christiana et naturalis*, grounded not
only in the Incarnation but its lowly matrix, grappled
the temporal by hoops stronger than steel to the eternal.
Yet it is organically allied to the pagan vision, as
expressed by Diogenes Laertius, of the Stoic philosophy :

> "The end is to act in conformity with nature, that is,
> at once with the nature that is in us and with the nature

of the universe, doing nothing forbidden by that common law which is the right reason that pervades all things and which is, indeed, the same in the Divine Being who administers the universal system of things. Thus, the life according to nature is that virtuous and blessed flow of existence which is enjoyed only by one who always acts so as to maintain the harmony between the daimon within the individual and the will of the power that orders the universe."

This lacks but one element in the interpretation of the natural law—God entering nature and living among those who lived nearest to nature :

> "O world invisible, we view thee,
> O world intangible, we touch thee,
> O world unknowable, we know thee,
> Inapprehensible, we clutch thee."

In the peasant's smock, not the priest's robes nor the king's purple.

In the stiff-leaf foliage of the pier-capitals of the Early English style as in the illuminated foliage margination of a Missal or Book of Hours, God, beauty, nature, work and man are all in harmonious relation. The capitals uphold the springers which uphold the vaulting of the house of God, so that nature comes right into the church and the functional is at one with æsthetic purpose. The sanctification of craftsmanship is perhaps the most significant contribution of the Middle Ages to the world, and agriculture was the empress of all the crafts. The spiritual order found its way into man's daily work, as the Son of Man had found his way into the carpenter's shop.

V. Natural Satanism.

The whole of the mediæval complex rests upon the natural law, both in its philosophical aspects, as exemplified in the quotations given above, and in the social and economic spheres, as exemplified in the Guild system, the country workshop, the peasant community of mutual aid and the feudal obligation. Yet, in the history of the Cistercians and that of the Papacy, we are witness in the later Middle Ages of a deterioration in its observance. It is this which renders the position of Aquinas of major importance. For what Aquinas did was to give a solidly realistic and philosophical base to the whole concept, first by defining the relation of the *jus naturale* to the *jus gentium*, secondly by swinging over the mediæval attention from Platonic idealism to Aristotelean realism, and, thirdly, by closing the division between the natural law and the idea of nature as the province of Satan. There was a danger in the appeal to Aristotle because his condonation of slavery and subordination of the individual to the State were entirely contrary to the principle of the mediæval natural law. But Aquinas was no blind Aristotelean ; on the contrary, as Aveling has pointed out in *The Social and Political Ideas of Some Great Mediæval Thinkers*, he reversed the Aristotelean position by reasserting the true value of human personality, the State being only the instrument for securing the liberties of the individual and preventing him from misusing them to the detriment of others. This is not the place to examine the relations of the Thomistic metaphysics to the realism of Aristotle, except in so far as the rather vague and inchoate Communism of the patristic definition of the natural law was now cleared up by affirming the reality of responsible property, while the Platonic repudiation of the senses was countered by Aquinas's insistence upon the philosophical implications of the Incarnation. As Chesterton wrote in *S. Thomas Aquinas*, the Incarnation was "a miraculous medium between heaven and earth," and so the Christian was a man who believed that deity had "entered the world of the senses." Aquinas "wanted the body and all its senses, because he believed, rightly or wrongly, that it was a Christian thing."

"For him (Aquinas) the point is always that man is not a balloon going up into the sky, nor a mole burrowing merely in the earth, but rather a thing like a tree, whose roots are fed from the earth, while the highest branches seem to rise almost to the stars."

Though I had not this passage in mind when I decided upon the title of this book, "The Tree of Life," I may perhaps venture to point out how compatible Chesterton's image is with it.

In *Seventeenth Century Background*, Basil Willey remarks, "During the Christian centuries Nature . . . had been consigned to the Satanic order." Since St Thomas was the chancel arch of the Christian edifice in the 13th century, this is a gross exaggeration. Had it been true, Christianity would have fallen into the pit dug for it by the Gnostics, the Manichæans and the Monophysites. But there is a partial truth in it. Both in Pauline and Augustinian theology the Puritan strain is evident enough, and it also appears in the celibacy of some of the early Christian marriages. Origen regarded the sexual life as in itself sinful and the occasion of sin, while the same Puritanism appears in Clement of Alexandria and Gregory of Nyssa. St Chrysostom spoke of women as a "divine calamity," and other instances are numerous enough to leave it in no doubt that it was a persistent strain both in patristic and mediæval Christianity. What a clarifying and integrating force, then, was the realistic philosophy of Aquinas, thrust up like a great rock between primitive Latin Puritanism on the one side and later mediæval Puritanism on the other! For the same strain, the same shrinking from the beauty of earth as the enchantment of the devil, the idea of nature as the fallen angel and the material world as the temptation of Satan subject to the divine malediction appears at the close of the mediæval period.[1] The *Imitation* of à Kempis will serve as an example : "If all visible nature could pass in review before thee, what would it be but a vain vision ? " Bertram Dobell, in his edition of Traherne, has pointed out the contrast between the isolation of the monkish ascetic from the commoners "in a transport of spiritual egoism" and Traherne's passionate enjoyment of the world of being :

> "Yet further, you never enjoy the world aright till you so love the beauty of enjoying it that you are covetous and earnest to persuade others to enjoy it."

The gentle-minded persuasive St Francis de Sales in *Introduction to the Devout Life*, written nearly half a century earlier than Traherne's *Centuries of Meditation*, takes up a middle position between the extreme opposites of Traherne and à Kempis. His exhortations harvest abundantly from the fields of nature in analogy and illustration, though much less richly than Jeremy Taylor's. The following is a fair example of his homely felicitous manner :

> "Do as little children do, who with one hand cling to their father, and with the other gather strawberries or blackberries along the hedges ; for, in like manner, while you are gathering and handling the goods of this world with one hand, cling fast always with the other to the hand of your heavenly Father, turning to him from time to time to see if your doings or your occupations are pleasing to him."

The bramble thorns here are by no means the hooks of temptation, so that the attitude of à Kempis cannot be called representative, as Basil Willey would doubtless claim, or exceptional. The general Catholic attitude

[1] It reappears in the somewhat Albigensian fear of and revulsion from nature in *Midnight Hour*, by "Nicodemus" (1942).

to nature has been in fact divided and so both consistent and inconsistent with its own natural law. It is probable that the heresy of Albi, which was war to the knife on nature, was largely responsible for this division. Though the Albigenses were exterminated, not so their doctrines, and the spread of those doctrines was a retribution for the savage butchery *en masse* of their adherents. The fear of nature in the Middle Ages is essentially Manichæan. The great achievement of Aquinas was by his mystical-philosophical system to remove this division.

How then did this division arise, and how comes it that the attitude of the Latin Church differed from that of the British Church, which never demonized nature, though its monks chose places to live in that would have driven the townsman out of his wits ? The answer surely is twofold ; the Roman Church was developed at the very heart of the Roman Empire, more urbanized than any previous Empire in the world's history, while the general decadence of the immediately pre-Christian world had transformed the pagan nature-deities into the *Di inferni*. Powicke, in *The Legacy of the Middle Ages*, says, "The lands around the Mediterranean were not merely full of superstition, they were entirely sophisticated, so that it was impossible to draw a sharp line between their superstition and their sophistry." It was thus only an unearthly and other-worldly religion that could have purged the world of city-states from the corruption and perversion of the existing natural religion. Its demonic viciousness, its unnatural cult of nature needed to be exorcised by prayer and fasting and by the appeal to a transcendent God who was not immersed in nature. The transition from abhorrence at these denatured nature-cults to a fear and suspicion of nature herself was but a step. But when Powicke goes on to involve the "rustic traditions" in this demonism and to fail to distinguish between a degenerate nature-

71

worship of principalities and powers and a divine Cæsarism that had hardly anything to do with nature at all, and the rural rites of the Virgilian scene, he falls into an error from which the British Church, crushing the "Druidic" thaumaturgy but living among and working with the peasants, was immune. So was Gregory the Great, whose wise decree was the purification of the heathen places, not commination, and when the pagan straw "dollies" that once were emblems of the corn-spirit and adorned the rick-gable or apex were made for the Harvest Festival (I know of three contemporary instances), the true Christian tradition, as launched by Gregory, was memoried and honoured.

Whether the Catholic Puritanism of the later Middle Ages and the Counter-Reformation was a survival or resuscitation of this demonization of nature by some of the Fathers or was the consequence of the growth of power-politics in the Church, it is quite certain that Puritanism, whether Catholic or Protestant, has always been the implacable enemy of nature, as by its urban origins Protestant Puritanism has always been hostile to the peasantry. The Renaissance was a humanist reaction against this Catholic Puritanism, as the Reformation gave it the hard and bitter form that appears in Milton's "foul deformities" of nature. The sense of the evil or illusoriness of the finite world also appears very definitely in Buddhism and in many of the later mystics, though not, I think, so universally as Reinhold Niebuhr (*The Nature and Destiny of Man*) claims for it. It was an error into which the inspired rationality of the great Aquinas never fell.

The idea of a diabolist nature latent or sporadic both in pre-Aquinan and post-Aquinan Christianity was an opportunity of which the Puritans of the Reformation took full advantage. And that its growth did coincide with the release of economic appetites (a kind of compensation) is sufficiently attested by the history of Puritanism itself in which hatred of nature coincided with the thoroughly worldly preoccupation with economic power. The 17th century fabric is woven of two contradictory strands, a recovery of confidence in a sacramental nature and a withdrawal from a demonic nature. But the dualistic split was implicit in the mediæval world.

CHAPTER FIVE

THE RECOVERY OF THE 17TH CENTURY

I. The Age of Reconciliation.

THE first half of the 17th century is easily the richest and most adventurous period in the literature, the thought, the philosophy and the culture of the English nation. Not the soundest—that best of all national attributes belongs to the 15th century, the golden age of the small man, the free peasant and the master-craftsman, like a serene but active garden of coral-making underneath the frothy surges of the foreign wars and the barons' wars and the dynastic upheavals.[1] By no means an assured and settled life like the England of the 18th century landed oligarchy, which in culture though not in power was an age of thus far but no further. Nor the most dominant in individual greatness, like the meteors of the 19th century shooting madly out of their social spheres in the vast murk of the new industrialism. But the age of the Shakespearean tragedy and its dreamy aftermath, of the great voyagers in strange seas of thought, of the prose cathedrals erected by Sir Thomas Browne and his peers, of the other-world brightness and fantasy of Donne and the Metaphysicals, of the country parsonage of Herbert, Herrick, Traherne and the Ferrars of Little Gidding, so sweetly blended of piety, poetry, scholarship and ruralism, of honey-

[1] Public life was at a very low ebb in the 15th century—witness the reign of the Machiavellian Richard III. But Eileen Power (*see later*) has left it in no doubt that this did not apply to yeoman and peasant England, and though torture was rife in higher circles, the witch to the peasant was still the "wise woman," not the satanic emissary of the 16th century.

74

tongued Marvell and the younger Milton, of the sons of
Ben, of the sacred-profane lovers who struck their lyres
of unearthly grace with elegant fingers out of laced
sleeve-cuffs, of the monumental theologians of liberal
Anglicanism, of the scientific philosophers, of the Gothic
classicists who made the Baroque style, of the poetic
wits, of the curious investigators and memorialists, of
the character-writers and last, but not least, of the
independent yeomen who made of their farms a cluster
of little commonwealths of earth.

In the 17th century, the *culture* of the English people
reached its golden and purple autumn, ripening all that
had gone before and crowded with promissory seedlings
of a spring to come. So far as the movement of creative
ideas is concerned, the 18th century, so beribboned and
belaurelled by the moderns, is; in comparison with the
17th, insignificant. It produced the perfect Englishman,
Dr Johnson, but little or no ferment of thought.

The religious culture of 17th century Anglicanism
had broken long enough with the Roman discipline to
avoid the hot-headed intransigeance not to say violence
of the youthful Reformation whose brutal repudiations
lost more for it than it gained. It was, therefore, a
period of consolidation and recovery on the one hand,
of choice and experiment on the other. It at once
initiated science and extended the humanism of the
Renaissance. Its free and ardent quest for the springs
of spiritual reality gave it a perspective of far horizons
that saw the past as a composition of varying contribu-
tions to be accepted or rejected according to the fullness,
but at the same time intensity of its own particular
insight. It was thus both daring and conserving in
spirit, liberal without that failure in discrimination
which marked the crudity of the Reformers. It absorbed
into its breadth of culture that part of the Renaissance
that seemed good to it, those aspects of mediævalism

75

that best suited its capacious soul and yet travelled beyond them both without resting content with what it found in either. It was a true autumn, as I have said, because it ripened and gathered the fruits of previous cultures and sowed and watered the bright shoots of a presaged spring, sweet, as Francis Thompson wrote, "with the unconceivèd wheat." It was an autumn too flooded with supernatural light. It stretched one hand back to the Gothic, primitive and classical past, all cultures radically different from one another and itself, and one hand forward to a scientific and philosophical future. For a moment it succeeded in moulding these heterogeneous elements into a plastic unity of its own.

Yet this exploratory spaciousness did not conflict with a fieriness of passion which found its expression in a new mysticism. Or, to use the convenient term repeatedly handled by E. I. Watkin in *Catholic Art and Culture*, the vertical movement of communion with God was enriched by the horizontal movement of discovering the intellectual treasure of this sumptuous world. Seventeenth century Baroque, for instance, was manifested in the Emblem Book or the formal and fantastic garden or the geometrical verse-forms of some Metaphysical poetry. It is thus, as Watkins has suggested, a classical expression of the Gothic soul, or, as it might be put, an attempt to suggest and contain and symbolize the infinite within a finite of ordered arrangement. Marvell saw that infinite reflected in his drop of dew, and indeed all the religious thought of this fermenting era strives for a meeting-place between the immanent and the transcendent, or, as Dorothy Sayers would express it (*The Mind of the Maker*), between the Fatherhood and the Sonhood of God.

Nothing, therefore, could be more untrue of this age than to call its religious poetry, as it has been called, pantheistic, that is to say, immanent alone. If, then,

all this experimentalism and width of range, this attempt
to combine fact with value, this strange trinity of the
Gothic, the classical and the mystical, this ransacking
of past ages combined with an eager scanning of the
future be considered in all its variety of manifestation,
and if at the same time the conserving of this most
cultured England be viewed in its collision with all the
dissolving and disintegrating factors that preceded the
Puritan Revolution, it seems that only one generalization
will fit its complexity. It is the Age of Reconciliation.

One of the symptoms of this reconciliation was a federal
alliance between religion, the beginnings of science and
poetry. The great age of poetic prose, of the poetic
attitude to life thus witnessed a recovery of the sense
of wonder. Since this sense of wonder was in itself an
expression of scientific curiosity, it was an enriched,
not a child-like, perception of what was admirable (in
the dual sense) in natural phenomena. This "admiration
and wonder," as Traherne called it, appears as freely in
poetry as in prose, notably in Donne, and, as was only
to be expected in an age whose grasp of scientific principle
was in embryo, allows for a good deal of credulity.
Basilisks, hippogriffs and other wonder-beasts, shrieking
mandrakes and other startling vegetation, crocodile
tears and other dramatic performances in the animal
kingdom, make this new world of the naturalist one
of illimitable adventure and strangeness. Nature was
still fairyland to these pioneers of exploration, but it
was a fairyland under observation and so no longer,
except among the peasantry, one of a memorial pagan
belief.

At the same time, this sense of wonder was definitely
an aspect of the religious mentality of the period, so
that the natural world was recharged with a sacramental
value. Basil Willey, in *Seventeenth Century Background*,
calls this a rebirth of confidence in nature, and Montaigne

77

finely epitomized it in : "Whoever contemplates our mother Nature in her full majesty and lustre is alone able to value things in their true estimate." Thus, at the outset, the period roughly from 1600 to 1640 confronts us with a new affirmation and a new synthesis. Donne's "Nature was God's apprentice to learn in the first seven days, and now is his foreman and works next under him," reclaims nature from darkness into light and recaptures her kingdom from the satanic dominion. It was the mediæval theory in a kind of Minority Report that chained Andromeda to the rock ; it was the 17th century Perseus that rescued her from the sea-monster. But this act of chivalry was a far more erudite and complex one than the simple gesture of love and understanding effected by primitive Christianity ; it was compounded of many factors, so that a corollary is to be added to the Age of Reconciliation. It was also one of non-specialization. It was an attempt at a structural unification of the mind and the senses, of society and nature under God, the poise of whose various elements was highly precarious and broke down under the shock of hostile forces.

II. The Poets and the Natural Creation.

The 17th century thus manifests what much later days have called a "return to nature," and if this has not been attributed to it as to the *Lyrical Ballads* of Wordsworth and Coleridge, it was because it was the movement of a whole culture, not of one small group, because it was fragmentary and defective and because it was multiform. The achievement of the Wordsworthian group is comparatively easy to comprehend as a reaction against the abstracted thought and stereotyped verse-forms of the immediate past and a protest against the expanding urbanisn of the contemporary world. It was a literary movement without the religious, scientific and philosophic complications of the 17th century consciousness, misunderstood from the very vastitude of its undertaking to affirm and at the same time to explicate the trinity of God, man and nature.

This "return to nature" is more luminously and transcendentally expressed in Henry Vaughan the Silurist, who has been called the precursor of Wordsworth, than in any other of the Metaphysicals. The point of convergence between them (their methods of expression are worlds apart) lies in their respective hunger for the unclouded vision of childhood, uttered by Wordsworth in *The Prelude* and *Intimations of Immortality*, and by Vaughan in :

> "Happy those early dayes ! when I
> Shin'd in my angel infancy."

and :

> "I cannot reach it, and my staring eye
> Dazzles at it as at eternity."

and :

> "An age of mysteries ! which he
> Must live twice, that would God's face see ;
> Which Angels guard, and with it play,
> Angels ! which foul men drive away."

and :

> "Man in those early days
> Was not all stone, and Earth ;
> He sigh'd for Eden, and would often say,
> 'Ah, what bright days were those !'
> Nor was Heav'n cold unto him ; for each day
> The valley or the mountain
> Afforded visits, and still Paradise lay
> In some green shade or fountain.
> Angels lay leiger there. . . ."

Now this is like Wordsworth's "from God who is our home," but it is also unlike, and enshrines a much more

79

complex because it is a profoundly religious feeling. For it is not merely a return to the primal innocence and perceptions of individual childhood, but to "that shady City of Palme trees" which is indistinguishable from St Brendan's Isles of the Blest. It is the return of corrupted humanity to Eden, the Eden sought by the saints of the British Church in elemental nature, the Golden Age of the primitive aspiration, the Land of Heart's Desire beyond the sunset and before the sunrise. It is a nostalgia for that radiant kingdom where man walked with God and which lies not in the future but the past. It is significant that Vaughan's mysterious poetry is shot through as much with images of darkness as of light :

> "O for that night where I in him
> Might live invisible and dim."

But it is a luminous darkness in which day lies hid. Except in so far as both were nature-poets and lovers of solitude and that Wordsworth read and learned from Vaughan, there is no resemblance between them.

Again, Vaughan flights back through his angel-haunted darkness to the visionary animism of St Francis :

> "He (man) knocks at all doors, strays and roams,
> Nay hath not so much wit as some stones have,
> Which in the darkest night point to their home
> By some hid sense their Maker gave."

This ultimate world in which beginning and end are one and of which sand, dust and stones "which some think dead" have more cognizance than man, is reached by the spirit as birds reach their spring-homes on migration. The old antithesis and antipathy between man, the child of God, and nature, the captured province of Satan, are reversed by those between God in nature and the artificial world of man:

Henry Vaughan

"The whole Creation shakes off night
And for thy shadow looks the light

. . . . .

All expect some sudden matter,"

and elsewhere,

"The rising winds
And falling springs,
Birds, beasts, all things
Adore him in their kinds,
    Thus all is hurl'd
In sacred Hymns and Order.   The great Chime
And Symphony of nature."

The poet identifies himself with this expectation of
enkindled nature :

"with what floures
And shoots of glory, my soul breakes."

by sheer force of meditative projection :

"When on some gilded cloud or floure
My gazing soul would dwell an houre
And in those weaker glories spy
Some shadows of eternity."

This order and harmony of nature are contrasted with
the human discord and restlessness :

"Settle and fix our hearts that we may move
    In order, peace and love,
And taught obedience by thy whole Creation,
    Become an humble, holy nation."

The sense of "grace" as a divine mercy bringing the
quiet of heaven to the vexed soul of man is extremely
strong both in Vaughan and in Herbert, and it is interesting that Niebuhr (*The Nature and Destiny of Man*),
though not referring it to 17th century mysticism,
regards it as

"the central issue of the Reformation, forgotten in modern elaborations of Protestant thought in which modern liberal Protestant interpretations of human nature and human destiny stand in obvious contradiction to the tragic facts of human history."

Vaughan's poetry is full of this idea of man finding refuge in the God of the still small voice from the futilities of his own self-will. Therefore, Vaughan is nearer to Shakespeare than to Wordsworth because the tragic drama of Shakespeare *is* one of self-will, the terror of its dynamism that rocks the creation and the outraged nemesis of the natural law which is Shakespeare's version of the still small voice. The Shakespearean contribution to this view of the universe I propose to develop later.

The most sanctified arts and pomps of man bear no comparison with the frequenting of nature by her own Creator :

> "No mercy-seat of gold,
> No dead and dusty Cherub, nor carv'd stone,
> But his own living works did my Lord hold
> And lodge alone."

And again it is the night that receives "God's silent searching flight" :

> "When my Lord's head is fill'd with dew, and all
> His locks are wet with the clear drops of night"—

the "dark Tent" whose peace is "seldom rent" except "by some Angel's wing or voice " or by some star "in sparkling smiles" descending "to lodge light and encrease her own." Hills and valleys no less than birds "into singing break," while stones are "deep in admiration" of that Providence who gave to all things their aptitudes and attributes. May-Day is a flowery welcome to this heavenly Adonis of the spring, while "the purling Corn" praises the Lord of the harvest, and the crowing cock "dreams of Paradise and light." The way to this

Paradise is through nature, through childhood, and through the morning freshness of early Christianity which Vaughan expressly mentions in his lightning phrase, "the youthfull world's gray fathers."

It is extremely signficant that Walton, in his life of George Herbert, draws special attention to the Rector of Bemerton's "primitive piety," while a fellow country parson and pietist of nature, Jeremy Taylor, drew his symbols and imagery as copiously from nature as Shakespeare did, The same tendency is revealed in Traherne's *Centuries of Meditation*. Like Vaughan he was a Celt by blood and like Vaughan breathes a nostalgia for the Eden "so divine and fair" in search of which St Brendan sailed into the sunset. He too "dreams of Paradise and light" :

> "The world is a mirror of infinite beauty, yet no man sees it. It is a Temple of Majesty, yet no man regards it. It is a region of Light and Peace, did not men disquiet it. It is the Paradise of God. It is more to man since he is fallen than it was before, it is the place of Angels and the Gate of Heaven."

Vaughan's "weaker glories" that shadow eternity are Traherne's "The sun is but a little spark of his infinite love ; the sea is but one drop of his goodness." Vaughan's "great Chime and Symphony of nature" becomes Traherne's :

> "The sun, and moon, and stars shine, and by shining minister influences to herbs and flowers. These grow and feed the cattle : the seas also and springs minister unto them as they do unto fowls and fishes. . . . None can question the being of a Deity but one that is ignorant of man's excellencies, and the glory of his dominion over all the creatures."

Traherne's feeling about man ("you are never truly great till all the world is yours") is nearer to Shakespeare's

The Tree of Life

"what a piece of work is man!" than Vaughan's "He knocks at all doors, strays and roams," but both are preoccupied with "Angel infancy," and Vaughan's "Birds, beasts, all things Adore him in their kinds" is Traherne's :

> "Therefore hath God created living ones ; that by lively motion and sensible desires we might be sensible of a Deity. They breathe, they see, they feel, they grow, they flourish, they know, they love. O what a world of evidences ! We are lost in abysses, we now are absorpt in wonders, and swallowed up by demonstrations. Beasts, fowls and fishes teaching and evidencing the glory of their Creator. Contemplate, therefore, the works of God for they serve you not only in manifesting him, but in making you to know yourself and your blessedness."

The sense of wonder is paramount in the Metaphysical poets :

> "How like an angel came I down,
> How bright are all things here" (*Traherne*).

They see the transcendental in the immanent, as Watkin claims for the Baroque art of this century. It does not appear again in English poetry until Smart's *Song to David* and Coleridge's *Hymn Before Sunrise in the Valley of Chamouny.*

> "Who bade the Sun
> Clothe you with Rainbows ? Who, with living flowers
> Of loveliest blue spread garlands at your feet ?
> God ! Let the Torrents, like a Shout of Nations,
> Answer ! and let the Ice Plains echo, God !"

This is the sense of Genesis at white heat but without the white sorcery of Vaughan's fey powers.

In my *English Countryman* I attempted to show that this most vivid apprehension of the morning of the world and of the primitive Church which lived with primordial nature was recovered by two country poet-parsons of the 19th century: William Barnes, the primitive Saxon, and Hawker of Morwenstow, the primitive Celt. The "return to nature" is also present in Marvell (who so oddly called himself a Puritan), though more sensuously as in the almost pagan rapture of *Appleton House.* It appears in Donne for all his excessively complicated nature, though more intellectually. Only in Vaughan is it a manifestation, in his most haunting lines, of almost pure spirit. In him it is an unearthly love of earth. All the mystical poetry of the 17th century is spell-bound by the sense of the Ancient of Days, of the sea of created, urgent being heard in the shell, or, as Marvell expressed it of his "orient dew,"

> "that drop, that ray
> Of the clear fountain of eternal day."

Godolphin, Henry More, Hall, Benlowes, Joseph Beaumont and Henry King were all transcendentalists who found in nature the immanence of the Holy Spirit— St Hildegarde's "fire of the Paraclete, life of the life of every creature." Henry More received particular joy from natural beauty :

> "The plants, trees and stones shed a constant though imperceptible effluence of their virtues for a certain distance round wherein, if we walk, we shall receive these effusions in their purity and enjoy the delightful operations of Nature's chemistry on our behalf."

A lower key but not out of tune.

III. Nature and Christianity in Shakespeare and Browne.
The same nostalgia also appears quite definitely in Shakespeare, though not in open acknowledgment. Yet the trilogy of last works, *Cymbeline, The Winter's Tale* and *The Tempest*, are haunted plays as Vaughan's are haunted poems. In them too shines the vision of

reconciliation and peace, not very different from Vaughan's

> "My soul there is a country
> Far beyond the stars."

"The style of Imogen," Charles Williams has written, "is the keynote of all ; the pardon of Imogen the pattern of all ; and both style and pardon, though so heavenly, are as realistic as anything in Shakespeare." In them the light of a wild and unsullied nature smiles upon the habitations of men ; in them the old Celtic world of fairyland floats like a tinted cloud upon our familiar earth and Prospero and Perdita move among scenes like those once trodden by the Saints of the Western World. And in this enchanted kingdom the timeless peasantry conducts its festivals and obeys the appointment of the seasons.

It may be said—this is but secular magic. Is it so ? Turn back a page of this great book of creation and what is *King Lear*, with its strange megalithic atmosphere, but a dramatic commentary upon the Sermon on the Mount—"The meek shall inherit the earth," if not our earth, yet the Kingdom of Heaven? The beyondness and yet the inwardness of that kingdom are all in the unearthly spirituality of that Lear who was once a towering peak of arrogance and pride, a very Jupiter among men who ends among the company of the Galilean he had never heard of. The great scene of the arraignment of Goneril and Regan as a pair of joint-stools by poor Tom and the Fool tremendously dramatizes "the first shall be last and the last first," as does Lear's

> "Thou rascal beadle, hold thy bloody hand,
> Why dost thou lash that whore ? Strip thine own back.
>
> .   .   .   .   .
>
> Through tattered clothes small vices do appear ;
> Robes and furr'd gowns hide all."

86

This compassion for the sinner and the poor, for, as Granville Barker has pointed out, "mankind itself" ("we come crying hither ; Thou know'st the first time that we smell the air we wawl and cry"), is combined with that fearful flaying of authority by agonized, mad, cast-out majesty. On a gigantic stage of elemental powers and presences, this compassion and this curse are a Renaissance version of what another King was to the Pharisees and what he was to the publican and the sinner. The "soul-making" of this almost superhuman figure in his savage realm; his passage from martyrdom to salvation through such dolours and terrors of evil, in short his "redemption," are as Christian a text as it well could be. The awful potency of evil itself is true to the Christian perception and the Christian tradition. The belief that evil is a figure of speech is indeed one of the more radical modern delusions. Events have been harsh to it.

Again, though Lear is restored both to his Cordelia and his right mind, neither of them live happily ever after, as would be the secular "solution" of the "problem." In other words, the whole point of the drama is the rebirth of Lear ; through the anguish and the humiliation he becomes a new man, almost you might say a new child. The accent of the play is on this act of regeneration, not on the recovery of his earthly kingdom but on his entrance into the heavenly one. This is Christian as contrasted with secular philosophy. I quote Niebuhr :

"The Christian estimate of human evil is so serious precisely because it places evil at the very centre of human personality—in the will. This evil cannot be regarded complacently as the inevitable consequence of his finiteness or the fruit of his involvement in the contingencies and necessities of nature. His essence is free self-determination. His sin is in the wrong use of his freedom and its consequent destruction."

Again :

> "The law of man's nature . . . is a harmonious relation of life to life in obedience to the divine centre and source of his life. This law is violated when man seeks to make himself the centre and source of his own life. His sin is therefore spiritual and not carnal, though the infection of rebellion spreads from the spirit to the body and disturbs its harmonies also."

Again :

> "The freedom of his spirit causes him to break the harmonies of nature, and the pride of his spirit prevents him from establishing a new harmony. The freedom of his spirit enables him to use the forces and processes of nature creatively ; but his failure to observe the limits of his finite existence causes him to defy the forms and restraints of both nature and reason."

I submit that this lucid definition is perfectly illustrated in the earth-shaking drama of *King Lear*. The sin of Lear is the pride of power ; the sin of Goneril, Regan and Edmund is that of a will-to-power which overrides the restraints and jangles the harmonies of nature. Goneril and Regan plunge the world into a moral darkness, reflected in the great storm. Their rebellion "spreads from the spirit to the body" and the order of nature is convulsed. The storm is the symbol of it and with the storm Lear's own inward frenzy is identified. This evil created by the misuse of the will passes through the world as a destroying flame but is self-destructive, and the redemption of Lear closes the dislocation and completes the Christian philosophy. Look upon this picture and on this. And the drama of *King Lear* is the drama of to-day ; the one is a dramatic, the other an historical interpretation of Augustine's "What could begin this evil will but pride, that is the beginning of all sin."

It is most clearly presented in the ice-cold passion of egoism in Iago, whose evil will to destruction has completely overcome the moral law : "Virtue ! A fig !

'Tis in ourselves that we are thus and thus.'' As Bradley
has pointed out, it is not so much envy as pride that has
bedevilled him, a devouring monomania of self-esteem.
He himself confesses to his will-to-power ("to plume up
my will in double knavery") as the motive, executed
with intellectual finesse and demonic artistry, for his
self-assertive triumph of destruction. With *Macbeth* I
shall deal later ; *King Lear* is sufficient for the moment
to illustrate Shakespeare's thought as a more Christian
presentation of reality than any Christian apologist
since his day has come within a hundred leagues of writing.
The plays of reconciliation that follow, with their fantastic
Baroque framework, are entirely true both to the Christian
ethos and the 17th century. They likewise reflect, as
also will be seen later, the "return to nature," as indeed
their creative art "itself is nature." The inclusion of
Shakespeare, the Stratford countryman, the creator
under the Creator, in a study of the relations between
Christianity and nature, is not merely relevant but
essential.

The position of Sir Thomas Browne is different in
degree but not in kind from that of Shakespeare and the
Metaphysicals. In his the sense of wonder and the
exploration of far horizons in the past are contained
but certainly not dwarfed by the detachment of the
naturalist and the antiquarian. Browne was indeed
the first of our great naturalists, but his scope was a
good deal wider than that of his successors. The modern
investigator does not wonder what song the Syrens
sang, what was the genus of the fishes caught in the
boat of the Saviour, and what were the habits of cocka-
trices. Nor did his scepticism, so curiously allied with
credulity, prevent him from swelling the chorus of
human recognition of transcendence governing the
immanent with the surge and reverberation of his mighty
organ of prose ;

"There are two Books from whence I collect my Divinity, besides that written one of God, another of his servant, Nature, that universal and publick Manuscript that lies expos'd unto the Eyes of all ; those that never saw Him in the one, have discover'd him in the other."

What Basil Willey enumerates as his large and comprehensive survey of "fable, fact, the Bible, the classics, science, theology, demonology, the schoolmen, pagan and Christian morals, sacred and profane love, activity and contemplation," is a supreme example of what T. S. Eliot has called "the unified sensibility" of the age. All were so many stops to pull out of his rolling and rhythmic sea of sound. Yet our Leviathan of prose was never caught in the hook of secularism :

"Pyramids, Arches, Obelisks, were but the irregularities of vain-glory, and wild enormities of ancient magnanimity. But the most magnanimous resolution rests in the Christian Religion, which trampleth upon pride, and sits on the neck of ambition, humbly pursuing that infallible perpetuity; unto which all others must diminish their Diameters, and be poorly seen in Angles of contingency."

IV. The Same in Milton and the Cambridge Platonists.

There are many differences between Bacon, Sir Thomas Browne and the Cambridge Platonists, but they are unanimous in attacking the mediæval Schoolmen for separating the created universe from its Creator. Basil Willey quotes Bacon's attitude to nature as the need to study its works as part of the duty we owe to the great Artificer of the world. He compares his anti-rationalist view with Wordsworth's "wise passiveness" and Keats's description of Shakespeare's "negative capability" in accepting the mystery of creation without attempting to rationalize it. Science was the humble and patient study of God's work as the supplement of his word. Bacon, he remarks, attacked the abstractions of the Schoolmen from precisely the same point of view as Maritain and Christopher Dawson in our own days have attacked the abstractions of scientific orthodoxy. Abstraction, whether religious or scientific, was the enemy. Here, again, the anti-specialism of the age is revealed, its passion for synthesis, the complexity of vision so richly orchestrated by Sir Thomas Browne which unites poetry with science, thought with emotion, fact with value, tradition with experiment, and law with imagination. So long as the divine interpretation of nature dominated the diverse literature and mentality of the age, separatism and so abstraction were kept at bay. At the same time, we find that the order of nature, the new concept of the "natural law," established by the everlasting "I AM," brings us in touch once more with the primitive Christianity of the British Church. Basil Willey brilliantly economizes this strain of thought as—

> "In its effort to throw off authority, the 17th century discovered an Ancient still older than the Ancients, in theology the Ancient of Days, in science Nature herself."

In contradistinction from Bacon, the Cambridge Platonists brought the human reason into the fold as a further reinforcement against this scholastic authority and the alarming spread of Puritan predestination. The alliance of philosophy with religion was an attempt to render into terms of an advanced mentality Christ's own "the kingdom of heaven is within you," expressed in John Smith's *Discourse* as "seek for God within thine own soul." This is Pasteur's "inner god" and the Quakers' "inner light." The danger, as Basil Willey points out, was to substitute the idea of a "deified right" governing the world of man and nature for the Person of Christ, the soul in nature, "natural religion" for revelation.

Such intellectualism that elevated concepts as the only reality opened the door to that very abstraction which in Descartes took mind out of matter altogether, and in Hobbes, the bitter enemy of the Platonists, turned nature into the Great Machine. Bacon made no such mistake with his sturdy triangle of God as the apex and Man and Nature the two base-angles.

The mistake of the Cambridge Platonists was surely to oppose idealism to materialism which, as Berdyaev has pointed out, was exactly the error of the crude and naïve Communist materialism in Russia. But Christianity is a realist and a personal Faith and so opposed both to materialism and idealism. Shakespeare the realist is nearer to the Christian essence than is the Platonic idealist who is uncomfortably near to Descartes, who debased the natural law which Shakespeare so tremendously affirmed. But the actual intention of Cudworth, More, Smith and Whichcote was to reunite mind with matter as their own philosophic version of the relation between transcendence and immanence, intuitively expressed by the spiritual genius of Vaughan and Traherne. "Mind," said Cudworth, "is senior to the world and the Architect thereof," and, again, even if perception can be analysed into motions (this is Basil Willey's abstract of Cudworth's argument), what of the *awareness* of those motions ? I may point out that Cudworth's priority of mind in nature is paralleled by Archbishop Temple's concept of mind as an emergence from nature but which alone can explain nature (*Nature, Man and God*). "If mind is part of nature, nature must be grounded in mind" :

> "In Nature we find God ; we do not only infer from Nature what God must be like, but when we see Nature truly, we see God self-manifested in and through it."

This is exactly the contention of the Cambridge Platonists.

But, Dr Temple adds, "this self-revelation is incomplete without the reality of Person," as William James expressed it : "turning the dead blank It of the universe into a living Thou." Personality being in itself a principle of variation, the Divine Personality asserts the variability of the natural order. But God transcendent is more than his actions in time and nature, and this "I AM" "is no variableness nor shadow of turning."

It was this depression of the Personal God that was the weakness of the Cambridge Platonists and opened the door to that abstraction which was completely to turn the "natural law" inside out and transform nature as the image of the divine into a predatory Juggernaut. Cudworth indulged a vision of the triumph of science—could he have foreseen, as Basil Willey remarks, what a box of mischiefs that dream was to unlock, he might well, like Prospero, have burned his books. The way was open to an ethical rationalism of the Marcus Aurelius type which did not take long to slough the adjective. In terms of concepts, the Cambridge Platonists reaffirmed the fiat of Genesis—"And God saw every thing he had made and, behold, it was very good." But they tended to translate the divine joy of God in his creation as the operation of the First Cause, and the doctrine of causality was to lead the human mind into dark and deep abysses.

Cambridge Platonism was, of course, a humanistic-religious movement, an attempt to synthesize the devotional or "vertical" (to refer once more to Watkin's terms) movement towards "the steep and trifid God" with the "horizontal" movement towards the discovery of the natural world. As an example of the synthesis, he gives the reader a thumb-nail sketch of Père Yves, the mystic with a passion for nature who comes nearest to our Platonists. "His attractive figure may well . . . . justify Christian humanism against Puritanism, Catholic or Protestant, which looks askance at man and nature."

Yet how perilous was the poise and how ominous the sullen roar of the incoming tide of Puritanism may be measured by another example of a 17th century Continental poet. He "expresses the divine love in the words and accents of Catullus," but has nothing but abuse for the passion such as that of the *Pastor Fido*, whose language and imagery he freely employs. Crashaw, who wrote of St Teresa as "my rosy love" and the Virgin as the "rosy princess," is the nearest English parallel. The sexual imagery of mystical ascetics is often indeed more repellent than that of the frankest sensualist. The Church, says Watkin, should have accepted the cosmic love of *Pastor* as the foreshadowing of a supernatural fulfilment, but what both Catholic and Protestant Puritanism actually did do was to cleave in twain the human Eros from the divine love and so the natural from the supernatural. Niebuhr has done great service to a right understanding of this vexed question by pointing out with his customary force and clarity the distinction between the primary and secondary attitude of Christian teaching towards the sensuous life. "If we discount," he writes :

> "Hellenistic theology with its inclination to make sensuality the primary sin and to derive it from the natural inclinations of the physical life, we must arrive at the conclusion that Christian theology regards sensuality as a derivative of the more primal sin of self-love."

And he quotes Aquinas : "The flesh is good, but to leave the Creator and to live according to this created good, is mischief." Puritanism and sensuality pursued as an end in themselves are thus the severed halves of one whole, each voraciously feeding on itself. The one led, as D. H. Lawrence has described, to a kind of longing for nothingness. The other was the forerunner of secularism in morals, as in its conception of human degradation it was the forerunner of State absolutism to control it, and in human affairs of the Economic Man.

The position of Milton is so ambiguous that he really eludes all definition. A Puritan but also a classicist, and so an heir of the Renaissance. A lover of individual liberty, yet one who believed and set down in marmoreal verse that knowledge was the source of all our woe. An upholder of the "godlike principle" in man and so anti-Calvinist, but, being convinced of natural Satanism, an anti-Aquinan mediævalist. Freer than the free Anglican Church in his defence of divorce, and yet a foe, like his co-religionists, to all expressions of sensuous beauty and a supporter of the iron despotism of Cromwell. He stands between two worlds, bestriding each as Antony did the ocean. His dynamic sense of individuality was obviously derived from the Renaissance, but how differently he regards the passion of self-will from Shakespeare ! Satan, as has often been marked, is the hero of *Paradise Lost*, and his rebellion, his will-to-power, is sympathetically handled by the Puritan revolutionary. It was better to reign in Hell than serve in Heaven.

V. *Heaven and Earth in the* 17th *Century.*

The heroic and benignant undertaking of the 17th century to build a Jacob's ladder between heaven and earth found yet another expression in the country parsonage. Here, removed from the envenomed controversy of the theological arena, it justified the Shakespearean "ripeness is all." I tried to give in my *English Countryman* a brief impression of its opulent culture, its autumnal maturity, its wisdom and tranquillity and its freedom of intercourse beween the sacred and the secular. In these country places won by husbandry from the graces of wild nature, quietism walked with holiness, as in a rugged tameless nature a thousand

years before holiness had walked with the great adventure
of conversion. I need not repeat here what I wrote
about George Herbert at Bemerton, the Ferrars at Little
Gidding and the "session of the poets," philosophers and
churchmen at the manor of Viscount and Lettice Falk-
land at Great Tew.

What I may usefully stress here is the liberalism of
thought and conduct with which the piety and learning
and literature of this rural priesthood was suffused.
Hales and Chillingworth, both familiars at Great Tew,
ranged freely from a mutual love of Shakespeare to a
free enquiry of all that is in heaven and earth, so long
as their talk was true to their kindred points ; Montague
declared for the "catholicity" of the English Church,
standing in the gap between Puritanism and the Papacy,
while Dr Gardiner said of the Prayer Book of 1662 that
"no formularies were drawn that gave so much liberty to
the human mind." Yet that breadth of mind did not
foreclose upon the mystical sense, what Andrewes
(quoted by T. S. Eliot) called "the word within a word,
unable to speak a word." It is needless to stress the
analogy in spirit between this inquisitive yet devotional
theology and the free-ranging mind of Erigena, between
the liberal Church of Donne and Jeremy Taylor and that
of Columba. Without Roman Catholicism, but also
without the Reformation, it could not have flowered.
But that flowering also owed much of its being to its
nostalgic dream of primitive Christianity.

But if these liberal and tolerant Academes of rural life
welcomed both scholarship and letters, art and philosophy,
as compatible with and a leavening of their piety,
yet dilettantism was absent from them. Not only did
Herbert practise the courtesy of "sweetness and light"
towards his villagers at Bemerton, but largely through
the influence of Laud anti-enclosure Commissions were
appointed in 1632, '35 and '36. The wave of the Tudor

Enclosures against the peasantry was stemmed and thrown back, nor were the village commonwealths molested until the Commonwealth broke up their patterns of play and festival, suppressed their folk-songs and dances and silenced the musical soul of rural England. Hammond and Steward, other churchmen who gathered to the hospitality of Great Tew, followed the example of Latimer and Crowley and preached against both usury and enclosure. Thus was the mediæval tradition of peasant ownership and peasant co-operation rescued from the brigandage of the Reformation by squire and churchman alike, asserting the one his personal, the other his spiritual leadership of the village community. "You are now," wrote Herbert to his wife :

> "a minister's wife and must now so far forget your father's house as not to claim precedence of any of your parishioners : for you are to know, that a Priest's wife can challenge no precedence but that she purchases by her obliging humility."

And the havoc to the rural structure caused by the absentee landlordism of the 18th century should be contrasted with Sir Richard Fanshawe's *Ode upon Occasion of His Majesties Proclamation in the Year* 1630, *Commanding the Gentry to Reside upon Their Estates in the Countrey.* For a few years between a troubled past and a yet more troubled future to come, religion, humanism and chivalry met together in peace and planted the standard of the good life in our native earth. For the English Church thus to have absorbed the Renaissance culture without forfeiting the Catholic tradition was a very great achievement.

Thus the 17th century affords as fruitful an example of wholeness in living and thinking as any age in any period of the world's history can equal. It absorbed into its own rich culture both the mediæval and the pre-mediæval past, accepting some elements and rejecting others. It restored nature to God and liberty to religion, and it tried to maintain a country civilization, at once native and traditional but recharged with new vital forces and sweetened with a humane and ripened culture. It was a culture built up from the transcendence and immanence of the Galilean Peasant, and it was based on a faith that had not yet abdicated its Christian and mediæval obligation to submit all temporal and secular phenomena to the test of the eternal law, which the Middle Ages called the law of nature. Even the Cavalier lyric, the most fragrant blossom of the 17th century secular Parnassus, is shot through with translunary gleams, while the Muse of Herrick plays the pipes of Pan in a Devon vicarage.

The Rector of Dean Prior seems to put only one foot over the threshold of the new age, partly because he drew more directly from the neo-classical Renaissance than his fellow-poets and partly because his inspiration was less complex. But those tender twilit numbers of his against the coloured sunset of a passionate joy in the passing reality of Merry England and the songs and dances of her festal folk are true 17th century. There are only two poets in English literature who authentically translate into their own individual idiom the soul of rural and peasant England—Robin Herrick and William Barnes, both country parsons. John Clare, though himself a peasant, or rather ex-peasant, is much more the meditative solitary and too near the grief of the dispossessed labourer ; Bloomfield, though he interprets the heart of the field-labourer, has lost the singing voice of the labourer's ancestor ; Wordsworth's was necessarily a sympathy detached from its cause. But Herrick sings the ritual, Barnes the workaday relation of the English communal village to English earth as very members of it. Herrick is pastoral England as it really was—both pagan and Christian. Herrick's idyllic country Muse of "maypoles, hock-carts, wassails, wakes," is certainly more pagan than Christian. We should be glad of it ; apart from the April felicity of his poems, his is a sane and wholesome corrective to the demonic view of our English peasantry falsely held by many of the religious, ancient and modern.

Nor did the culture of the 17th century lack organic roots. As I attempted to demonstrate in a previous book, it was the golden age of the yeoman free-holder, while I also gave evidence for the claim that it was the 17th century, not the 18th, which was the great age of discovery and experiment in husbandry, frustrated and suspended by the Puritan Revolution. The English yeoman was always a religious man, and it can truly be said of him that he husbanded his land with a devotion that was in essence a sense of spiritual responsibility.

So also with natural history. That great scholar of nature, John Ray, the fountain-head of the long stream of English naturalists in the field, and, indeed, the precursor of natural science, regarded the exploration of nature as a means to interpreting the logos of Deity. He expressed his own synthetic view in unmistakable words :

> "There is, for a free man, no occupation more worthy and delightful than to contemplate the beauteous works of nature, and honour the infinite wisdom and goodness of God."—(*Translated from the Latin by Dr C. E. Raven.*)

Thus, from the cultivation of the land upwards to the subtleties and refinements of philosophic speculation, from the great craftsmen of regional building, of textiles, ware, wood, glass, iron, straw, pewter, silver, enamel and leather to the prose of the Bible and the dramatic poetry of the Jacobean playwrights, from the greatest prose to the greatest poetry, the 17th century up to the

Commonwealth reveals the Christian Faith in dynamic contact with English earth. A survey of this difficult period unfolds it as an attempt to translate into multiform action the words of M. B. Reckitt in *Faith and Society*:

> "Amid all speculation and controversy upon the significance of the kingdom in Christ's teaching, the inevitable conviction emerges that it included the idea of the earth intended to be and capable of becoming the scene of a Divine Order."

But the disruptive forces were too strong and the quest magnificent was stayed.

CHAPTER SIX

THE SEPARATION OF NATURE FROM RELIGION

I. Nature as the Great Machine.

"SUBSTITUTION of the spiritual for the material," wrote Alexis Carrol in *Man the Unknown*,

> "would not correct the error made by the Renaissance. The exclusion of matter would be still more detrimental to man than that of mind."

Before nature could *become* "matter" it had to be excluded from the fold of God the shepherd and man the flock and so play the part of the wolf that preyed upon it. A wolf indeed, the neo-Darwinian wolf and the wolf of David Hume which has taken the place of Gregory of Nyssa's serpent which tempted Eve. The transformation of nature from the tent of God to which stars or angels hastened down "to lodge light and encrease their own" into matter was the achievement of the 17th century. Or, as Prof. Whitehead wrote in *Science and the Modern World*:

> "Nature is a dull affair, soundless, scentless, colourless, merely the hurrying of material, endlessly, meaninglessly. However you disguise it, this is the practical outcome of the characteristic scientific philosophy which closed the 17th century."

But that is only half of it. In becoming mechanical matter, nature also became a devouring dragon. How was this possible ?

This revolution was the work of Hobbes, who degraded man below his true level, and Descartes, who elevated

101

him above it. The modern world is the creation of Hobbes, Descartes and a watered-down and twisted version of the Christian tradition. Progress, a modern invention, has consisted in the gradual elimination of the third partner. Hobbes fathered the idea of the totalitarian State and Descartes was responsible for thinking of all life in terms of abstraction, or, as we put it, of "problems" and their "solution." The influence of both was entirely subversive and revolutionary ; they destroyed the primitive, mediæval and 17th century conceptions, differing in degree but not in kind, of the natural law. Their example equally excluded God from his own universe. The modern experiment is thus foredoomed to failure because it has cast itself loose from the spiritual and natural foundations that alone can hold it firm to reality.

If I study the transformation of the natural law in England rather than more generally in Western Christendom, it is because in England it was more dramatic. England possessed a tradition of liberty in unison with a passion for the land which, if not unique, was incomparably more organic and deep-seated than among her fellow-Christian nations. The authentic English culture has always been individual, independent and linked with a love of nature that, so long as it lasted, kept it realistic. Even to this day it is so when that tradition is in mortal struggle with absolutist forces not only from without but most dangerously from within. The drama lies in the new philosophy cutting right across this tradition of the real, the Christian and the natural England.

Tawney, in *Religion and the Rise of Capitalism*, has described the most momentous change to the modern world as "the secularization of political theory," and Hobbes and Descartes are quite definitely the two gateposts of philosophy between which the old world passed into the new. By the time of the Restoration, he says, the Tudor clash between Christian morality and economic interests has been decided and the theory of the application of a Christian standard to economic conduct had surrendered. Theology surrendered to ethics, ethics to economics, and man followed suit from a spiritual being to an economic animal. The terms of surrender are indeed explicitly set out by the Tonnage Act of 1694, by which the king handed over his prerogative in the issue of money to a private interest in the newly created Bank of England. Thus the Bank of England took precedence of the Church of England by relieving economics of Christian supervision and giving it into the charge of itself. The mediæval idea that it was right for a man to seek the wealth necessary for his livelihood in his particular station but wrong for him to seek more, and that that kind of enterprise was the sin of avarice, was dissolved in the acid of an expediency that could not but justify usury as the legitimate exercise of self-interest.

The Reformation was undoubtedly responsible in part for this enormous change and, but for the recovery discussed in the last chapter, would have been so in whole. The Tudor Enclosures, which, as Sir Thomas More said, made sheep the devourers of men, was a purely predatory movement of land-speculation and gambling in wool on the part of the town against the country, and so precipitated the change. The mediæval doctrine was acceptable to a society of small masters and peasant farmers who practised an ethic of mutual aid and regulated their exchanges by the just price. The Tudor merchant and privy councillor who bargained with the monastic lands like a stockbroker with bonds was in his war against this society depriving ownership of its mediæval safeguard as trusteeship and substituting competition for gain in place of co-operation for livelihood. This social and economic revolution, checked by a complex of tendencies already examined, was completed by the commercial bias of Puritanism whose issue was the Tonnage Act.

But the successive phases of the great change from what Tawney calls the idea of society as a spiritual organism to that of society as an economic machine were themselves accompanied by a philosophic revolution that separated nature from religion. Hobbes and Descartes were its instruments, and John Locke was the intermediary between them and the Cambridge Platonists. It was impossible for society to be conceived as an economic machine, moved by "the pulleys and levers" of economic self-interest, until nature had become the "Great Machine" of matter in perpetual motion. There was an autumnal quality about the Cambridge Platonists, and the work of Locke was that of the first frosts which prepared the way for the full winter of *Cogito ergo sum* and the *Leviathan*. Once nature ceased to be the created of the Creator—and Hobbes was an atheist whose "religion" was mere window-dressing for keeping on the safe side of public opinion—there was nothing for it, and "it" is the right word, but to become a gigantic spinning-top.

II. Locke's Idea of Nature v. Shakespeare's.

What Locke did (his attitude is well explained by Basil Willey in *17th Century Background*) was to translate the mystical mind working in nature of the Cambridge Platonists into a kind of sweet reasonableness in which the order and harmony of nature were carried over into the order and harmony of science. The result was that nature did quite literally get left out in the cold, since science is not nature but an abstraction from nature. Locke in consequence does not really know what to do with nature who, or rather which, becomes an unwanted guest in the neat edifice with modern furnishings and amenities of the first of the planners. Nature becomes an inconvenience, and this is actually the word that Locke uses—"the proper remedy for the inconvenience of the state of Nature." Nature, once permeated by the divine reason, has reason taken out of her, a reason now humanized which looks back on nature not as a wicked but an awkward step-mother. The *mens sana*, leaving nature, is safely lodged in the *corpore sano.*[1] Locke's idea of Deity—and deity is still present though in a transitional state—reconciles science with religion, not nature with religion. But God and nature are now worked out on evidence, not experienced by communion, so that their demonstration rests on mathematical principles, and the great 18th century antithesis between reason and enthusiasm or inspiration has been conceived in the womb of a common sensible philosophy. Keats in his lament for the fading-out of the sensuous world "at a touch of cold philosophy" might have headed it "John Locke."

Metaphysical poetry faded out with it—stars that came eagerly down to make candles for a Lord whose locks were wet with the clear drops of night were now about their proper business of geometrical revolutions. Shelley succeeded in being a poet of abstractions, and Hardy wrote a mighty epic upon "Necessitation," but the Metaphysical poets of a rejoicing Genesis could not square their visions with what Toynbee has acutely called "the apathetic fallacy" of enlightened common sense. Poetry, to cite Willey once more, tended to become "pleasurable fiction by truth being handed over to

[1] The change-over from tradition to the new philosophy Basil Willey (to return to him) finds expressed in Wren's architecture. But Wren is nearer to the Baroque than Locke is to Cambridge Platonism, and the Baroque as aforesaid (*see* p. 76) is an attempt to reconcile the Gothic with the classical. Wren was not so close to the Gothic as Shakespeare, but his buildings are still far from the cold and alien formalism of the haughty Palladian mansion.

philosophy" and, finally, I may add, "the picturesque," a word invented by a rational divine (the Rev. William Gilpin) of the 18th century. This meant poetry (and those parts of nature that were not "horrid" like downs and heaths) not only separated from imaginative truth but from real life. Poetry as ornament or what Sprat called "the devices of Fancy or delightful deceit of Fables" was as far away from the storm in *King Lear* as Deism was from God. Abstraction not merely exiled God from earth but (this is the important point) man too. The modern idea of both poetry and nature as a playground to which man comes from the distance of more serious occupations was born. In Vaughan the concrete is never separated from the visionary, the realistic from the transcendental.

Shakespeare once more comes in here to illustrate the theme, which is that of abstraction dividing God from nature and man from both. If we look at Shakespeare over against Marlowe, the apostle of the Renaissance "Glory to man in the highest," and Whitman, we come to understand this disintegration from a new angle. Whitman was one of the least regional of poets. He did not confine himself to a single continent. He was the "world-citizen"; his eyes were fixed on the horizon rather than on the ground at his feet, and he embodies in his own American fashion the spirit of expansion. The sense of mass, of speed, of size, of distance, of "the conquest of nature," of vastness and capaciousness, all these distinctive elements of the modern spirit are foreshadowed in Whitman.

Shakespeare affords a dramatic contrast with Whitman which can be expressed in a sentence : while Whitman was cosmopolitan and abstract, Shakespeare was regional and universal. His approach to life and to human nature was realist, based on his own observation and the same kind of experience as Vaughan's of God-in-nature. The principle upon which his imagination worked was contractive, individual, selective, organic, not expansive, generalized, abstract. He worked always from the particular to the universal, and when the very globe seemed to be wrenched off its axis by the power of evil as in *Macbeth*, the firmament to be convulsed as in *King Lear*, these paroxysms of nature were rooted in *this* castle and *that* storm on the heath. None the less, the storm was universalized, as Vaughan universalized a waterfall, a dead tree, the purling corn. In Shakespeare all is personalized, even when he is drawing upon the stock-in-trade of his contemporaries or is uttering conventional sentiments, and the grandiose standardization of Whitman would have been as abhorrent to his creative and qualitative spirit as was the cloudy rhetoric (which he parodied) of Marlowe.

As a rural memoralist, Shakespeare enormously surpassed the whole of his contemporary playwrights, whose statistical records in this respect are extraordinarily poor and insignificant. Country imagery in Marlowe, for instance, is very rare indeed—Marlowe the townsman, the doctrinaire Machiavellian, the poetic imperialist, the lover of "huge cloudy symbols," who drew his current account from the empyrean, hardly at all from the earth. Shakespeare's regionalism (of which there are scores of examples) and concrete rural warmth of suggestion are utterly different (as Dr Caroline Spurgeon has pointed out in *Shakespeare's Imagery*) from Marlowe's temperamental choice for lunar, solar, astral, firmamental imagery, cold and majestic and abstract.

The magic of his last three plays is a country magic and their spirit is of a Gothic and primitive past from which he had never been wholly separated, so that his own aerial visions were blended with rustic jollities and rural traditions of fairyland. He had conquered the world but he returned to his own place. He went back home but his poetry had never really left it. The restlessness (so like what Vaughan was always referring to), the cosmic feverishness, the sense of size and mass, the ideological abstractions of Whitman were never his, not because he lived more than two centuries earlier but because he was a poet with roots in his own land whence he drew his mighty strength and enriched the garden of his home. Shakespeare could never have been what Dryden called "the man who of all modern and perhaps ancient poets had the largest and most comprehensive soul," had his unparalleled genius not been nourished in the rural tradition of what Henry James called "the core and centre of the English world, midmost England, unmitigated England." What is still more to the point, he could never have dramatized the heart of the Christian Faith as he did in *King Lear,* had he not in his own heart and mind belonged to that integrated world which Hobbes and Descartes cleft to the chine.[1]

III. The "Natural Law" of Hobbes and Descartes.

We are thus able to appreciate something of the

---

[1] The country imagery of Shakespeare covers a very wide field—birds and animals, the weather and the seasons, clouds and the sky ; the river Avon on whose banks he was born ; country sports and games ; wild flowers ; husbandry ; a large number of rural crafts such as smithying, pottery, coopering, knitting and embroidery, and particularly carpentering ; the activities of the farm kitchen and— by far the most abundant and varied—gardening. The plays and poems are stuffed with horticultural analogy and illustration, sometimes, of course, borrowed from Pliny and the herbalists of the time, but so often precise and exact that they must have emanated from his own personal observation and predilection. And his lines about the lace-makers of the Midlands sitting at their cottage doors in the evening sun weaving their bobbins (as I used to see them) :

"Mark it, Cesario, it is old and plain (the folk-song) :
The spinsters and the knitters in the sun,
And the free maids that weave their threads with bones (bobbins)
Do use to sing it."—

are in the same notation of rural realism as "Consider the lilies of the field."

magnitude of the revolution which they set in motion and which has collapsed, burying half mankind under the debris, only in our own time. What Wordsworth called the "meddling intellect" of Descartes generated, indeed, one of the greatest revolutions in ideas the world has ever known. It was a revolution against a tradition of more than a thousand years' duration, and Basil Willey suggests that Vaughan's and Traherne's nostalgia for childhood was a revolt against the Cartesian contempt for history and the past of the human being. For to Descartes childhood was "error." Equally "erroneous" to him were Augustine's famous words (quoted by Una Ellis Fermor in *Masters of Reality*) :

> "Ye have told me of my God, that ye are not he ; tell me something of Him. And they cried out with a loud voice, 'He made us.' . . . These things did my inner man know by the ministry of the outer : I, the inner, knew them ; I, the mind, through the senses of the body."

But with Descartes nature and the senses were but "extension." Only the mind *was*.

What he did was to elevate man above his proper station, above, that is to say, his "creatureliness," by his intellectual gospel of egocentricity. "I am," he wrote, "because I think." Neither God nor "I" were realities, both being intellectual abstractions whose activity was not in acting nor being but only in thinking. The only certain thing about them both was the mathematical method of arriving at this conclusion. It was the mind not the senses and emotions which perceived the external world, extended through infinite space and controlled by mechanical laws. The one reality was just "I," and even that was only a mental proposition. Basil Willey says that the Cartesian cleavage was between values and facts, between what you felt and what you thought— Donne and Sir Thomas Browne having felt and thought

109

simultaneously. But in isolating values from facts, Descartes virtually destroyed both. For facts only become real in so far as they are observed, and valuable in so far as they are experienced, and the Cartesian method was contrary both to observation and experience. The only reality was the mind's concept of itself as a mind, a mind torn out of the body which was a concourse of atoms in motion. Mind floated in a void ("extension"), neither of which had really anything to do with the other.

A lonelier thing is not conceivable, cut off not only from the past, from the great tradition built up out of the Incarnation between St Paul and Shakespeare, from sensibility (surely Descartes banished the poets more effectively than Plato), but from everything except itself. It cannot even be conceived how it got there, the Cartesian ego, since it could not have arisen out of the atomic whirl. There it just was, and yet the there was a nowhere. The Cartesian mind is, as Dr Temple remarked in *Nature, Man and God*, a solipsism because it ignores the kinship between the mind and the nature which gave rise to it. Thus the mind finds its other in the object to which it is akin. This otherness, continues Dr Temple, is

> "an unambiguous affirmation of transcendent Mind, apprehended by reason of its Immanence in nature, physical and spiritual."

But in Descartes there is no kindred Otherness at all.

If to Locke nature was an inconvenience and God what Matthew Arnold called "a power not ourselves making for righteousness," that is to say, an edifying text, the mind or ego of Descartes was suspended in sheer nothingness. Chesterton's definition of a lunatic—"A lunatic is not a man who has lost his reason ; he is a man who has lost everything except his reason"—might well be applied to Descartes' mental ego. It was hardly surprising that, when science took full charge, mind too was expelled from this new universe. For the exaltation of reason meant the death of the soul. "When we say the 'self,'" wrote Father D'Arcy in *Death and Life,*

> "we mean much more than the mind ; we are composed of body as well as spirit, and our body enters into the act of thinking. We cannot, in other words, call our thought our own, our own consciousness, unless the senses and our psycho-physical organism play their part."

Hobbes was an altogether coarser type than Descartes ; as abstract as his co-destroyer he had nothing like his intellectual refinement. He was the most worldly of all our philosophers and his concepts were always coloured by his cynical temper, given full weight by the structural power of his prose. If atomism and mechanism were by Descartes restricted to the "extended" world but excluded from his "I," with Hobbes the matter-motion complex was all. That all was "but one universal cause, which is motion." The interesting thing is that these "motions of the mind " as well as of the external world are conceived in terms of passions, or rather appetites, whose purpose is power. Thus Descartes' egocentricity becomes Hobbes's egoism, and all life, while still a mechanism, is a cockpit of contending selfish desires, purely anarchic and so—here he switches on to the political theory for which he has been notorious for three centuries—only to be restrained by the superior force of Leviathan or the autocratic State. Since the natural state is one of incessant strife and rapacity in which the weakest can only overcome the strongest by fraud or guile, and "every man is an enemy to every man," the only possibility of some kind of a social order is by the imposition of it from the supreme sovereignty of the State.

It is not possible to conceive a more radical repudiation

111

of the natural law which, with backslidings and constant interruptions of deed but not of deliberate mental sabotage, had held the allegiance of Western man since the 2nd century. The whole conception is every bit as abstract as Descartes' : the natural war of all against all is a mere notional premise, unsupported even by Descartes' "evidence" ; taken for granted, the rest follows. Nor does Hobbes attempt to explain the immunity of Leviathan from the predatory passions it exists to harness and balance ; that immunity, lacking which its purpose is self-defeated, is taken for granted, like the premise on which it was founded. Abstraction could go no further. It has in it a diabolically sublime simplicity in the most violent contrast with the complexity of his age—"all that is real is material ; and what is not material is not real"—could anything be plainer than that ? It is as simple as darkness in which the shapes and relations of things are not seen.

Hobbes has always been acclaimed as a great logician, and yet there is no true logical connection between his nature as fate, man as automaton and the exercise of those furious passions that only absolutism can control. For how can the will-to-power exert itself without that free-will which Hobbes abolished ? How can a machine generate the emotions of lust and domination ? A machine is not a chaotic assemblage of parts. In spite of this *non sequitur*, it is in Hobbes that appears that interrelation between determinism and natural predacity that has bedevilled thought ever since the publication of *Leviathan*, whose mixture of philosophy and science was to become a witch's brew. United with Descartes' self-deification of the ego, these Three Furies have swept through the world like a devouring flame. "It is the cause, it is the cause, my soul"—it was the idea, the abstract idea which was caught up by Mandeville, Malthus, Adam Smith, Comte, Huxley and the neo-

Darwinians, all the heirs in their different qualities and degrees, some in one way, some in another, of Hobbes and Descartes.

In Toynbee's *Study of History* there is a section devoted to what he calls the nemesis of the idolization of the ephemeral self, of, that is to say, the Hobbesian and Cartesian abstractions put into practice. He ranges from the idolization of a political sovereignty in a human being as illustrated by the Pyramid Builders and the Roi Soleil; from the pride of Jewry with its paranoia of the "Chosen People" that accepted the Father and rejected the Son to the self-infatuation and sacred egoism of Periclean Athens that came to play the part of the jackal to the Roman lion; from the Aztecs, Assyria, Mycenæ, Macedonia, Rome, Carthage, to the Cæsaro-Papism of the Eastern Roman Empire which transferred its worship "from the Creator to the creature." The doom of the strong man armed, the successive suicides of the Tamerlanes of history is his text, of all those States or conquerors or power-fanatics who have asserted the egocentricity of Descartes or the absolutism of Hobbes. Ranging from Sargon and Rameses to the "predatory plutocrats of the 19th century" (and a further extension is obvious), he describes what happens to societies which allow themselves to be ruled by men as gods. Was it, he asks, the war of extermination against the Albigenses that precipitated the downfall of Catholicism? "Has not Time," he asks again, "been fattening our Western body social, like a sacrificial victim, for a mightier holocaust than Orthodox Christendom was ever able to afford?" From Hubris to Nemesis one civilization has followed another into the abyss. Whenever "the glory of the uncorruptible God has been changed into an image made like to corruptible man," Hobbes's Fate has followed Hobbes's natural law. The greatest drama of man's self-worship that has ever been written, the drama of *King Lear*, has been the drama of civilization.

Hobbes and the Puritans were of opposite parties in the Civil War, but it is obvious that Hobbes's determinism was in close alliance with Calvinist predestination. And just as Hobbes's idea of nature as the "Great Machine" was linked with his idea of natural predacity, so his theory of State absolutism proved compatible with the opening of the career of economic individualism. Cromwell's was an absolute government, but it was in Cromwell's dictatorship that the man of business began to bestir himself. Defeated in the 15th century, checked during the period of the early Stuarts, he was launched on a very long voyage by the Puritan Revolution.[1] Everywhere the voyage was convoyed by a fleet of scientific philosophers armed either with economic theory, evolutionary biology, mechanistic physics or Freudian psycho-analysis. "The unspeakable horrors of the Aztec sacrifices," wrote Aldous Huxley in *Beyond the Mexique Bay*, "were a logical outcome of the cosmological speculations of a few philosophers."

IV. Spengler's, Hardy's and Huxley's Idea of Nature v. Shakespeare's.

The sense of the inexorable that is so clearly derived both from religious predestination and secular determinism expressed itself in both pessimistic and optimistic forms. In Hobbes, it is wholly pessimistic, whereas the tolerant, hedonist, sceptical, enlightened self-interest of the 18th century took on the whole a cheerful view of life. Indeed,

---

[1] It is interesting that Rochester, in his *Satire on Man*, directly attacked the Hobbesian fallacy :—

> "Thus old age and Experience, hand in hand,
> Led him to Death and made him understand,
> After a Search so painful and so long,
> That all the Time he had been in the wrong."

Mandeville's idea (*Fable of the Bees*) that "man's self-interest is God's Providence" was a comfortable way of making the best of both worlds—if your interest happened to be in the ascendant. For the unpropertied poor who, according to Malthus and Adam Smith, were only deserving if they were submissive and possessed nothing to sell but their labour, Providential good cheer was less conspicuous. The 18th century theory of absolute rights was for him who could get hold of them. Cheerful on the whole, but there was Swift whom savage indignation drove mad, Hogarth whose vision was hardly roseate and Dr Johnson who was anything but an optimist. There was the fashion in necrology that spread like wild fire from Blair's *The Grave* and Young's *Night Thoughts*. The root of 18th century rational complacence was insecurity, as indeed history has demonstrated. Young's *Night Thoughts* was to become Thomson's *City of Dreadful Night*, and a half-contemptuous tolerance of balanced interests to creep into the self-styled philanthropy of the "dark satanic mills" and explode into a totalitarian intolerance seventy times seven more tyrannous than the Inquisition. Freud's is a strange compound of hedonism reacting against Victorian prudery and dutifulness, and pessimism reacting against the fatuous optimism of Victorian automatic progress. Jung's *Modern Man in Search of a Soul*, by its brilliant and very definite repudiation of the Freudian subconscious of the primeval slime, almost embraces the Christian philosophy. But the Freudian *libido* is but another translation of the will-to-power whose nemesis was for all time revealed by Shakespeare, and the "infantile-perverse-criminal" unconscious derided by Jung is a modern rendering of the Hobbesian primitive-predatory anarchism. H. G. Wells's wicked old man of the tribe is plagiarized from Freud.

Spengler's determinism was equally a pessimistic

reaction against the myopia of the progressivists, based upon a revival of the Greek idea of cyclical recurrence and periodicity. Spengler's great canvas of the inevitable doom that attends one civilization after another from the biological cradle to the grave, from youth to senility, is simply a graph of the curve of predestination, an abstract diagram of the natural automatism. The process is not evolutionary but seasonal. But it is still Destiny, the substitute for the Fatherhood of God. How man can be thought and machine at the same time is best known to the modern children of the Hobbes-Descartes parentage. The biological life-cycle is the wheel that moves the cart, but, as Toynbee has remarked, the cart can only go where the driver wills, and the driver is the divine creative spark. The spark that equally redeemed Lear from his downfall and circulated the sap of life through a Renaissance which created Michael Angelo's Adam on whom God looks down but without touching his outstretched arm—the perfect example of man's free will operating under a divine supervision that is not interference. Here, writes Watkin, is "the truth of human nature, of history and religion, natural and revealed." But it is not the truth of Spengler's wheel of Sisyphus, of Puritan predestination, of Hobbesian determinism, of Shavian vitalism, of Rousseau's immanence and of Victorian progress. They may all be said to culminate in the hedonistic but despairing determinism (a queer mixture) of FitzGerald's rendering of *Omar Khayyam*, the pet of the Edwardians :

> "We are no other than a moving row
> Of magic Shadow-shapes that come and go
>   Round with the Sun-illumined Lantern held
> In Midnight by the Master of the Show ;
>
> But helpless Pieces of the Game he plays
> Upon this Chequer-board of Nights and Days . . .

The Jacobin Idea of Nature

O Thou, who Man of baser Earth didst make,
And even with Paradise devise the Snake :
  For all the Sin wherewith the face of Man
  Is blackened—Man's forgiveness give—and take."

The Wilderness with the girl and the flask of wine is
exactly the same place as Thomson's 'Dreadful Night.

Nothing, again, could have been more abstract than
the Jacobin *droit naturel* which, like other abstractions,
revealed its true nature in practice by the mowing off
of heads in the name of liberty, fraternity and equality.
Rousseau's *Social Contract* with its view that institutions
had debased man's natural virtue was, of course, a reaction
against the Hobbesian natural predacity and so went
some way to reaffirming the mediæval natural law. It
was thus in sharp conflict with the view of the Encyclopædists who regarded nature as necessity in which (to
quote Niebuhr) "the will to live of competing organisms
had established a kind of equilibrium." So Holbach :
"The essence of man is to love himself : thus interest
and desire are the only motives of all action." The
theory of abstract rights came to dominate the French
Revolution partly because of this purely materialist
conception and partly because Rousseau was a deist,
not a Christian—his Supreme Being was immanent,
not transcendent. And immanentism is always the
parent of abstraction, of the indefinite rather than the
infinite, while history shows that abstraction and barbarism so often make good bedfellows. It was only a
step from the identification of deism with the *droit
naturel* to the expulsion of God from nature. Once God
was expelled from nature and nature was no longer a
divine ordinance, nature and man, her child, became
automata and there was nothing else for it but that.

It is clear, as I have said, that the Puritan sense of
man's degradation is as generic with Hobbes's anarchy
of appetite as is their predestined with his determined

man, and Tawney has brilliantly and with finality analysed the development of a predatory commerce from the Puritan matrix. Benthamite utilitarianism and the economic *laissez faire* of the 19th century were derived as historically from Puritanism as they were conceptually from the Hobbesian clash of competitive powers. The early Shelley (*Prometheus* strikes a deeper vein) was an inspired leader of the romantic revulsion from the 18th century version of Locke's common sense, but both he and the 18th century rationalists were abstract and Utopian gospellers of human perfectibility. That in itself is only one more of the philosophic renderings of "Glory to man in the highest, For man is the master of things," which Descartes bequeathed to the world. The optimistic restraint of the 18th century in due time expanded into the optimistic licence of 19th century economic piracy, driven by the determinism of Progress and padded by the respectability of Puritan moralism. Against this Thomas Hardy's pessimism in its turn reacted but only to assert a sterner, more inexorable fatalism than Calvin himself. His Spirits of Pity are the ineffectual protest of Hardy's own profound humanity against the senseless automatism of the Demiurge.

Since Hardy was also one of the very greatest of our ruralists, it is worth while examining the immense paradox which his division of artistic being imposed upon him in accepting nature with his spirit and mechanizing nature with his mind. Because of this radical contradiction between intuition and intellectual abstraction, there is no imaginative writer in our language, not even Blake, who offers such formidable difficulties to final evaluation as this old-fashioned serialist, this tremendous humorist of folk society, this greatest of rural regionalists, this recording angel of the first shadow of Europe's eclipse. The inevitable worm he discovered at the heart of the universe was a very different worm from the one his earth-sense was aware of as sweetening his Dorset soil. "The village atheist brooding over the village idiot" was the same man who dignified all humanity by making (like John Langland of *Piers Plowman* before him) shepherds and woodsmen giant symbols of ever-lasting truth.

Perhaps the greatest paradox of Hardy's tragic muse is that it is not inherently tragic at all. In the Shake-spearean sense of the term, the essential element in tragedy is lacking from the black flag running up from Tess's prison, from Sue Bridehead's child swinging from the beam, from the very "Immanent Will" itself or rather It-self. The evil will-to-power of Goneril, Iago and Macbeth is a far more profoundly tragic conception than "an automatic sense Unweeting why or whence" on whose unconscious designs the impersonated spirits in *The Dynasts* brood as they watch the clash of nations, "supernatural spectators of terrestrial action." Human beings are necessarily its pawns, whereas in Macbeth, in Hamlet, even in Ophelia and Cordelia, who seem only flies to the wanton thumb of the President of the Immortals, there is conflict and duality. Even Cordelia has a certain tart inflexibility (a chip of the old block) that not diminishes her glory but contributes to weaving her own fate. There would be nothing tragic in Macbeth if the Immanent Will had propelled him to the bedside of Duncan, the passive instrument (as Napoleon is repre-sented in *The Dynasts*) of the unconscious It "whose fingers play in skilled unmindfulness." The Shake-spearean tragedy is vitally one of a flawed humanity whose free will offers it dualistic choice. This *is* the Christian doctrine which Hardy rejected, and the experi-ence of history overwhelmingly confirms it as authentic.

The Christian doctrine of free will is indeed the axle-tree of the Shakespearean tragedy. Napoleon the chess-board piece of Fate but not Macbeth of the Witches.

119

The ambition of Napoleon is inexorably decreed ; the ambition of Macbeth is a passion of evil will within himself, struggling into a monstrous growth against the impulses of loyalty and imagination. The very intensity of that sombre imagination reinforces the true aspect of the crime as a spiritual perversion. There is conflict even in the "unsexed" Lady Macbeth :

> "Had he not resembled
> My father as he slept, I had done't."

The evil influence from the Witches reaches both Macbeth and Banquo ; the one succumbs to it but the other keeps "my bosom franchised and my allegiance clear." Banquo is present with Macbeth on the blasted heath (it is a desert place, not an ordinary heath, be it noted) for the express purpose of the contrast between the one's rejection and the other's reception of the withcraft.

In *The Dynasts*, Fate and Nature are fused into Necessity that drives Napoleon like the engine the machine. In *Macbeth*, the Three Witches, the floating dagger, the mysterious Third Murderer, are symbols and emanations of the evil principle within the soul of Macbeth himself and tenebrously within the world. But they are *not* derived from nature. The evil-doer is himself explicit in acquittal :

> "Thou sure and firm-set earth
> Hear not my steps, which way they walk, for fear
> The very stones prate of my whereabout
> And take the present horror from the time."

Macbeth has murdered sleep, "great Nature's second course," and the earth, appalled at the violation of the natural order, "was feverous and did shake," and,

> "Thou seest, the heavens, as *troubled with men's act*,
> Threaten his bloody stage."

Witness, again, Coleridge's comment on Macbeth's distraction on seeing the ghost of Banquo at the feast : "He has by guilt torn himself live-asunder from nature, and is, therefore, himself in a preternatural state." Bradley (*Shakespearean Tragedy*) repeatedly declares that Shakespeare took pains to underline Macbeth's full responsibility for his own deeds. Yet most inconsistently he finds in the lines :

> "Lamentings in the air, strange screams of death
> And prophesying with accents terrible,"

evidence of nature being "sympathetic with human guilt and supernatural malice." It is surely clear that the meaning of the lines is precisely the opposite. These instances—and there are others—are evidence enough that neither necessity nor nature drove Macbeth to sacrifice his "eternal jewel" but his own choice. And that is the Christian as opposed to the modern view, the realistic as opposed to the abstract. Lastly, the evil is recognized in *Macbeth* for what it is ; in *The Dynasts* it is but It. Therefore, among the other phenomena of modernism we have to reckon the loss of the tragic sense. For Hardy's idea of tragedy is definitely pre-Christian and pagan : its theme is the enmity of the gods to man.

Is Huxley's "unfathomable injustice of the nature of things" a tragic conception ? Certainly not and in fundamental philosophy Huxley and Hardy are interchangeable. Tragedy is absent alike from the "drowsy knitter" insensately manoeuvring the "flesh-hinged manikins" as bobbins to interlace the meaningless fabric as from the manikins themselves. If we look upon Hardy's philosophy both of life and of not-life as a man of genius's poetic distillation of a social automatism, an economic determinism and a religious predestination that preceded them, we find him not only the most eminent but the

most representative of Victorians. The social structure
of the Victorian era was built up on Hardy's "Necessitation sways," while its favourite "law of supply and
demand" renders into economic terms that pervasiveness
of "chance and change" which saturates his shorter
poems. He was regarded as a spearhead of rebellion
against Victorian ethics and conventions. And that of
course is true of him as the man, the poet and the artist.
But it is certainly not true of him as the conscious
philosopher. Not the least of his many-sided achievements was to have caught and transfused through the
alembic of his powerful and sombre imagination the
philosophical implications of Victorian thought, derived
from the Hobbesian and Cartesian break with the tradition
of eight centuries. "Necessitation sways" is own brother
to the Marxian "Historical Necessity," just as the deified
racial State is to the deified Socialist State. Hardy's
thought interprets modern thought ; it certainly does
not rebel against it. The dualism is in Hardy himself,
not in his presentation of tragic themes ; it was the
tragedy of paradox between his intellectual system and
the deeply traditional intuitions of a warm and loving
nature.

The concept of free will in which the Shakespearean
tragedy was rooted is as richly charged with tragedy and
dynamism as it well could be, and both Hardy and his
age offered an inflexible alternative to it. It is therefore
one of the ironies of literary history that Hardy's anti-
Christian bias was directed against the formality, the
respectability, the complacence, the caste system, the
Puritanism of Victorian Christianity, and so its protection
of social injustice. It is singular indeed that this prescient
mind, for whom the beauty of nature and of human
character in organic relation with nature and with
Wessex were so fiery a passion, should have substituted
for human volition and the intercourse between man

and God the notion of "a sublime fermenting-vat" as the grand original of the cosmic process. And with a truly sublime resolution he boiled in it all his life. Not for him that other offshoot of religious predestination and economic determinism—the downright imbecile doctrine of Progress. He stood inside but also outside his age in that he predicted that universal catastrophe which has devastated the world, the fruits of that false philosophy to which he himself was in bravest bondage. The greatness and creative power of Hardy reside in his interpretation of man's relation to his native earth, at once realistic and symbolic. That it should have emerged in all its beauty and splendour through all the impediments of style and language he imposed on it and in spite of the polar creed he wedded to it, is a measure of how great that greatness was.

V. *Nature as Anarchy and Mechanism.*

Just as Hobbes's collision of furious appetites is worked in with his mechanization of the universe, so Hardy's fatalism is at one with accidentalism and Huxley's passionless atomism is on perfectly good terms with the ferocity of "the ape and the tiger" in human affairs. The "law of the jungle" was in harmony of discord with "the law of supply and demand," both with "this thing the world by chance on atoms is begot," and all with automatic progress. Huxley's distortion of the Darwinian natural selection into a gangster film made the "cosmical process" responsible for the predatory individualism of his age, as though a process were capable of exerting a human malevolence and rapacity, as though an abstract conception had horns and a tail. Huxley, indeed, our scientific Calvinist, actually cited Hobbes in his attempt to prove that it is in our stars, not ourselves, that we are underlings and that the "cosmical process" was a gigantic Victorian age, the "continuous free fight" of the "gladiatorial show." As Adam Smith's *Wealth of Nations* made the acquisition of riches the key to national welfare, so "the survival of the fittest" became the dominance of the greediest who were able to gratify their most spacious ambitions by the exploitation of backward countries and the discovery of cheap power by and through the Industrial Revolution.[1]

Nor yet had the curse of Hobbes and Descartes, the Dioscuri of the Dawn of Progress, worked out its full logic upon mankind. The Cartesian abstraction generated the impersonal combine out of individual gainfulness, and the piratical commerce of the *entrepreneur* gave way to the diabolic holiness and mystery of a financial priesthood. This corporation of what might be called absentee shareholders developed out of Locke's own joint-stock company which was responsible for the South Sea Bubble. The word "Bubble" is indeed of enormous significance ; the Cartesian and Hobbesian philosophers blew out a great abstract bubble which they called the universe. A. J. Penty, in *Tradition and Modernism*, has an amusing example which reveals how the same unreality has come to be attached to money. If a halfpenny were put out at interest on the first day of the Christian era, it would now amount to an octillion, an amount in bullion equal to several gold spheres as big as the world. When money thus breeds money, it becomes in itself a kind of world-bubble—but full of explosives. Indeed, the Black Magic of finance, whose dictatorship ("no one can breathe against the will of the financial dictatorship"—the Pope in *Quadragesimo Anno*) has supplanted even that of big business, is a perfect example of the lengths to which false theory can carry the foolishness of man. "We are betrayed by what is false within."

[1] A sharp and clear distinction should be made here and below between trade and mercantilism, industry and industrialism.

Business enterprise which had displayed certain human qualities of adventure and resource and vitality began to look to a bureaucratic technocracy as the best means of achieving its ends. Men turned into masses. Nature, the Great Machine, supplied the example for the mechanization of humanity. Nature the Tiger had been so suicidal as to afford man the spirit and the means for "the conquest of nature," the slogan of science. This phrase, "the conquest of nature," one of the most baneful in the history of the world, is indeed a paraphrase of Hobbes's "lords and possessors of nature." At the same time, science, forgetting that a generalized animal in nature succeeds where a highly specialized one fails, carried abstraction to such a point that it split up into minute specializations, got rid of the "life" factor which the biologists had left intact and put chemistry in charge of the organism. To describe a phenomenon in abstract terms was to explain it and master it. One side of the Hobbesian philosophy, the mechanistic, came to be considered as a cure for the other, the acquisitive. Thus, the remedy for individualism was State absolutism, for anarchy power-politics, for exploitation organization. Adam Smith's notion that government must not interfere with natural laws has developed into something like State capitalism. The German State that Hobbes would have applauded as controlling individual rapacity is itself more predatory than anarchy itself. Abstract terms like "democracy" came to mean the rule of a minority by means of propaganda and the power of wealth over vast aggregates with a collective way of life and a collective "soul" pent up in squalid industrial cities.

An internationalism imposed from above (and so abstract) became the tenth-rate substitute for the universal that the old world had seen in the particular. "Labour well the minute particular," as Blake said. But this internationalism, and the uniformity which was a symptom of it, did not exclude the most violent hatreds and rivalries and beggar-my-neighbourliness in perpetual combustion. Thus, a contentious cosmopolitanism, as M. B. Reckitt has pointed out in *Faith and Society*, is linked with the dehumanization of industry by appealing to an automatic law of supply and demand which never works and conducting its finance by tiny, anonymous, all-powerful groups utterly remote from actual production. It is a curious example of the blindness to which abstraction leads that the "Manchester School" believed an expansive industrialism to be synonymous with peace. Gregory, as Toynbee remarks, made no such error. He built up from a solid religious foundation, not on economic sands and sordid economic interests.

The quantitative production of goods in the mass became a virtue in itself, regardless of their quality, the uses to which they were put and the inability of consumers or purchasers to buy them. A "virtue of necessity" to keep the huge Moloch of mass-production going as a condition of full employment, a condition incapable of fulfilment. The idea of home, the most real and concrete of actualities, succumbed to the enchantment of distance and the intoxication of expansion. The obsession with size and system assumed that ills occasioned by them could only be medicined by a larger edition of them, and that a defective machine could only be set to rights by an efficient Machine. At the same time the machine, still following Hobbes's connection between automatism and appetite, was tied to profit, and in this phantasmal world, "efficiency" came to mean practically the opposite of itself, not making a good thing but a good thing out of a thing that might be good but was more likely to be the reverse. Thus far the world had travelled from the mediæval ban on usury, rooted, as Toynbee said, in the idea that economic activities were means not ends in themselves. Nothing could be more abstract than the idea of gain for gain's sake, unless it be work for work's sake regardless of its character or aim.

VI. The Apostasy of the Churches.

How did the Church withstand this cataract of anti-Christian, anti-natural and anti-realistic philosophy? The answer is that, swept down by the tide which in the first half of the 17th century it had so valiantly resisted, it found itself half-drowned in a backwater out of the main stream, surrounded by moral reeds and sententious sedge. "The most surprising result of the Revolution of 1688," wrote Charles Marson in *God's Co-operative Society*, himself a country priest, "was the withdrawal of our clergy from the political and social spheres." Newman wrote in *The Arians of the Fourth Century*, "The Church was formed for the express purpose of interfering with the world." "Compromise," wrote Tawney in *Religion and the Rise of Capitalism*, "is as impossible between the Church of Christ and the idolatry of wealth, which is the practical religion of capitalist societies, as it was between the Church and the State idolatry of the Roman Empire." His further acid comment on "the abdication of the Christian Churches" from interfering with the theory and practice of the philosophy outlined in this chapter I quoted at the beginning of the first chapter.

Not for the modern Church was the martyrdom of the primitive one. Its spiritual impotence and inertia were indeed so complete (with the partial exception of the campaign against negro slavery) that it is to be wondered that Huxley ever bothered himself to flog the prostrate form of the dormant donkey. A conventional pietism, a set of moralistic precepts, or, what Tawney called the inculcation of such "personal virtues as did not conflict" with plutocracy, were its alternative to it where it did

127

not, as in the Enclosures, actually co-operate with it. The social values of Christianity were partially upborne through the flood by such as Goldsmith, Blake, Cobbett, Coleridge, Ruskin, William Morris, Samuel Butler, Dickens and Chesterton.

To this apostasy and defeatism there were exceptions, and I described a number of them among the country clergy in my *English Countryman*. To them should be added men like Wesley, Newman, Manning, Gore, Scott Holland, Stuart Headlam, Westcott, Marson and others, and, in our own days, Temple, Widdrington, Demant, McNabb, D'Arcy and others, catching up the Isaiah-like pronouncements of a noble line of Popes. The heroic slum priests of the 'sixties and 'seventies were preceded by the Tractarians and a true spiritual movement gained weight and momentum from about 1850 onwards. But it lacked any real understanding of the social situation created by the Industrial Revolution and the philosophy behind it. The Oxford Movement quite failed to formulate a Christian sociology, though the Guild of St Matthew and the Christian Social Union strove to do so.

But there were and are two phenomena that militated against the effectiveness of these undaunted bodies and undaunted individuals. Unlike the mediæval canonists and the 17th century clergy, they were no longer articulating and interpreting a common loyalty, an accepted truth, a Christian society. They were in arms against their own age. Secondly, they failed, except sporadically, to bring into action an affirmative, realistic counter-philosophy to that degradation and exploitation of nature which germinated and spread a dark satanic wing over the whole world from the egg that was hatched by the incantations of Hobbes and Descartes.

Suddenly, the whole crazy edifice fell to pieces. But man, sitting or dying among his own ruins, still did not weep as his forebears had done by the waters of Babylon.

He did not "dream of Paradise and light," as Vaughan had done, but of Utopia, a plan-made Paradise on paper. He was still Monarch of all he surveyed, only what he surveyed were ruins. Yet an uneasy voice within himself, a still small voice, was whispering to him that the reign of Hobbes and Descartes was at an end. Or, as Berdyaev has put it, "the end of our time." The end of the colossal experiment to get on without the conception, common to art, poetry, craftsmanship and theology alike, that "the word was made flesh and dwelt among us."

The Titan achievements of the modern world are their own panegyric. Their value for mankind and the life of the earth has been largely (though not altogether) vitiated by the bad philosophy that caused them to be misused and converted them to energies of waste and destruction. Its untruth is the concern of a later chapter, but it is partly disclosed already by the radical contradiction between turning nature into a machine and man into a thinking-box without any logical or organic connection between them.

CHAPTER SEVEN

THE DECLINE OF THE PEASANTRY

I. The Permanent Peasant Values.

IN the second chapter, an attempt was made to describe Galilee, the birthplace of God, as the meeting-place between the heavens and the earth, between the two extremes of transcendental kingship and the labour of the fields. But it is only by witnessing as a whole the social and economic consequences of the decline of the peasantry, the foundation-stone of all civilization, that an inevitable conclusion emerges. Even if the Incarnation of Christ be mythological and if his life as a peasant, living the peasant life, practising a peasant craft and uttering the peasant speech, was an historical accident and not the purpose of the divine wisdom, human society would be compelled, not merely for its salvation but its self-preservation, to sanctify the organic relationship of the peasant to the earth. The historical record of the Incarnation is, in fact, among other issues a consecration, in terms of supreme Personality uniting eternal truth with its temporal expression, of that very necessity. In other words, the justification of the New Testament as a country chronicle lies in the fatality that attends human history when civilization becomes detached from the security of the peasant values and the stability of its peasant origins. Peasant economy is the ground-floor of the structure of civilization ; industrialism but its top-heavy upper storey.

Nor can those values be rightly apprehended unless the craftsmanship inseparable from the peasant community is contained within them. Just as Descartes slashed mind out of the womb of nature, so modern perversity has hacked Art (with a capital) out of craftsmanship. Both these arbitrary cuts are anti-historical and contrary to the nature of reality, and God the modern Mathematician is an absolute which lacks that intimacy with man and nature which God the Divine Craftsman whose Son was a carpenter fulfils.

The previous chapter travelled from the ancient world of realistic to the modern world of abstract conceptions, from the idea of nature as a creation to the idea of nature as mechanism. This one follows a parallel course from the integration of society to its disruption and from the conservation of the earth to its exploitation. The interacting philosophies of Hobbes and Descartes marked the transition in thought ; the change-over from subsistence to capitalist farming marked it in social and economic practice. A third line of advance has been that of "the conquest of nature." In the interests of commerce and that science attached to commerce, it has rifled the world of its natural fauna and flora, reduced and potentially exhausted its natural resources, dislocated its natural balances and violated its natural beauty. It thus belongs to a category which includes both theory and practice and is therefore allied to the one form of transition and the other. In a century and a half, raptorial man, by his enormous destruction of the higher forms of life, has brought almost to a close the Age of Mammals that began in the Jurassic period.

It is not surprising that religion, crushed between these steel rollers, ceased to be the bread of ultimate reality and emerged as the lifeless dough of a sanctimonious nonentity. The root cause of its own mechanical pietism has been stated by P. E. More :

> "The most insidious and obstinate enemy of religion was, and is, the subservience of the mind content to see in this world only a huge fatalistic mechanism or a

131

heterogeneous product of chance, or, as the modern Darwinians would have it, a monstrous combination of both. Whatever form the error may take, it is devoid of the logos as the creative wisdom and purpose of God, a magnification of the creature, a refined but at the same time devastating species of idolatry."

But, as the part played by our own clergy in the Enclosures which destroyed our peasantry and the overwhelming urbanism of modern Protestantism and Roman Catholicism clearly demonstrate, religion suffered as deeply from the decline of the peasantry as it did from the philosophic mechanization of nature. It would seem impossible to separate the degradation of nature and husbandry from the lifelessness of religion.

"The parish," wrote AE, "is the cradle of the nation," and this statement of basic reality is paralleled by Charles Marson's summary of its true anatomy :

"We find man as part of a family, the family as part of a tribe or shire, the tribe part of a nation, the nation part of a group division, the group division part of the great human stock."

The self is the starting-point ; the family enlarges the self ; the tribe keeps the family from being introvert and exclusive ; the nation enlarges the bounds of the tribe and common nature is above all, through all and in us all, "which is the very portal of God." You build, that is to say, from the bottom upwards, according to the natural order, not from the top downwards, according to the modern system. The idea of the Holy Family is thus a symbolic representation of the nature of human society. Just as the craftsman works with the grain of natural substance, so the community of families that forms the village works with the grain of life. Or, as Montague Fordham puts it in *The European Peasantry*, 1600-1914 :

132

"The peasant outlook and the peasant philosophy
. . . came from a remote past, and may arise from
some essential element of human life."

The manorial village in its turn, like the relation
between master and apprentice, translates into common
and earthly terms the conception (*see* Chapter III) of the
Good Shepherd of the Catacombs. Leader and led, in
spite of theological abstraction, is, as Middleton. Murry
has rightly pointed out, a fact of human nature. It is
when master and man are united in a common work and
a joint responsibility that life unfolds itself from bud to
flower in the village community, the craft-workshop and
the town-guild. The proper relation between master
and man has been perfectly expressed in Sir Thomas
Overbury's "Character" of a yeoman :

"Though he be master, he says not to his servant
'go to field' but 'let us go,' and with his own eye doth
both fatten his flock and set forward all manner of
husbandry."

Place, that is to say nature, is the binding condition of
each nucleus, both as a social organism and a vocational
group. A nomadic community, hunting or pastoral,
may change places, but they are still places, and civilization decided that place was better than places.

So long as these communities remained local and
organically knit together, so long as the local "lord"
(once the village leader) or priest or master-craftsman
was bound to members of the community by his responsibility for them and a common share directly or indirectly
in the natural wealth, society remained a stable organism
capable of the richest possible developments. I need
not repeat here the historical account I gave in my
English Countryman of our English peasantry as a nexus
of local communities achieving a balance between individualism and common ownership which was both

and neither but a thing in itself. The lord of the manor fitted into the village complex so long as he did not abuse the trusteeship which the mediæval natural law regarded as obligatory, and, though the squire virtually destroyed the peasant in the 18th and 19th centuries, there is no doubt that in previous ages his leadership was very often both the motor and binding force of the community. At the head of this work I placed a quotation from Tawney's *The Acquisitive Society* :

> "Whatever the future may contain, the past has shown no more excellent social order than that in which the mass of the people were the masters of the holdings which they ploughed, and of the tools with which they worked. . . . With this conception of property and its practical expression in social institutions those who urge that society should be organized on a basis of function have no quarrel. It is in agreement with their own doctrine since it justifies property by reference to the services which it enables its owner to perform. All that they need ask is that it should be carried to its logical conclusion."

This traditional, democratic and local self-government did not suffer from its graded and hierarchical order so long as it was co-ordinated on the one hand and elastic on the other, so long, that is to say, as the worker on the land could become an owner of it and the apprentice in the workshop a master-craftsman without disturbing the equilibrium of a co-operation dictated by the common need. Property was the condition of freedom, mutual service in a common task in one place ("thou shalt love thy neighbour. . .") the condition of its creative function. Propertied rights were customary so that the preservation of liberty depended like the craftsman's work upon traditional inheritance.

At the same time, the obligatory services that the individual land-holding peasant exchanged with his fellows

134

in the village-farm he owed and paid to the land itself.
The conservation of the land by rendering back to it
what its fruitfulness yields in the endless circulation of
organic and vegetable residues is as much an axiom of any
community of peasants and yeomen (the aristocracy of
the peasantry) as it is the law of nature's own fertility.
The peasant's relation to the land is symbiotic *by nature*
and so the reverse of predatory. Lastly, peasant society
is invariably religious, whether Pagan or Christian, and
so tenaciously religious that a new religion is hard put
to it to replace the pagan substratum. The Peasants'
Revolt of 1381 was passionately Christian, but the peasants
who revolted possessed a folk-memory that went further
back than Christianity. The author of *Piers Plowman*
"saw Christ walking in the English fields in the dress of
an English labourer." Fordham, in the same paper as
I quoted from above, picks out three characteristics of
peasant society in all ages and countries—realism, constructive thought and mysticism. Thus, the hallmark
of every peasant society is that of integration between
nature and religion, freedom and tradition, responsibility
and ownership, social service and individual rights.
That such wholeness was commonly realized in practice
would be too much to claim ; what is incontrovertible is
that it was the normal and familiar pattern of peasant
society, especially, be it noted, in Saxon, 14th, 15th and
17th century England.

It is most unusual to find a modern intellectual com-
prehending, much less accepting this wholeness of peasant
society. But there is one who so does, the most distinguished of them. Aldous Huxley, in *Beyond the Mexique
Bay*, writes :

> "So much for what civilized man cannot take from
> their primitive neighbours (what he calls the 'negative
> good taste' of peasants). What *can* they take ? They
> can take, or at least they can try to take, the primitive's

(he means peasant's) human wholeness. A primitive (*viz.*, peasant) is forced to be whole—a complete man, trained in all the skills of the community, able to fend for himself in all circumstances ; if he is not whole he perishes. . . . A highly organized society protects him (the civilized man) from the worst effects of his own incompetence ; allows him to be ignorant of all the useful arts and yet to live."

This is the most brilliant of urban minds seeing through urbanism, but that urbanism is revealed further on in the book by the author's defence of peasant craftsmanship as only a negative counterpoise to the vulgarity of modern urban and popular art. It is therefore not to be upheld for its æsthetic value which is so-so, but as a social utility of the "highest value." It is "essentially inferior" to the work of the great artist. Well, of course, who would contend that the structure of Flatford Mill was as great a work of art as Constable's painting of it ? But Huxley, though not openly saying so, leaves the impression that folk-art is different in *kind* from what is called the work of art. Eric Gill did much good work in exposing this fallacy, but a hundred instances expose it yet more effectively. Here is only one. I have, for instance, a yew armchair made for me by a village craftsman only known to a few which is hardly distinguishable from a Chippendale of which it is not an imitation. And what of an exquisite work of art like the Geddington Cross which stands in the village of that name ? It is as great a work of statuary as anything by Pheidias or Praxiteles, but it is a product of folk-art. The difference between folk-art and great art is, of course, a difference in degree, not in kind, for, as Eric Gill truly said, quoting from A. K. Coomarswamy : "The artist is not a special kind of man, but every man is a special kind of artist."

II. *Changeless Craftsmanship.*

Turn to the craft-guilds, recruited from the country workshops, of the market-town which was in relation of mutual exchange with the cluster of villages in its neighbourhood. They too reflect in being and in function the early Christian interpretation of the natural law. Theirs too was a brotherhood under the Fatherhood of God. I quote from A. J. Penty's *A Guildsman's Interpretation of History:*

> "There can be little doubt that it was because the Guilds of the Middle Ages were pervaded by religious sentiment that they were so successful as economic organizations, for we must not forget that the sense of brotherhood and human solidarity was restored to the world of Christianity after it had been broken up by the growth of capitalism under the Roman Empire. This sense of the brotherhood of mankind made possible the Just Price which was the central economic idea of the Middle Ages. It was an idea unthinkable in Rome, where conquest and exploitation seemed but the natural order of the universe. The Just Price left no room for the growth of capitalism by the manipulation of exchange, for it demanded that currency should be restricted to its primary and proper use as a medium of exchange. . . . Only by the exercise of authority over its individual members could the Guild prevent profiteering in its forms of forestalling, regrating, engrossing and adulteration. Trade abuses of this kind were ruthlessly suppressed in the Middle Ages. . . . But a Just and Fixed Price cannot be maintained by moral action alone. If prices are to be fixed throughout production, it can be done only on the assumption that a standard of quality can be upheld. As a standard of quality cannot finally be defined in the terms of law, it is necessary, for the maintenance of a standard, to place authority in the hands of craftsmasters, a census of whose opinion constitutes the final court of appeal. In order to secure a supply of masters, it is necessary to train apprentices, to regulate

137

the size of the workshop, the laws of labour, the volume of production, and the like. . . . It is thus that we see all the regulations—as indeed the whole hierarchy of the Guild—arising out of the primary necessity of maintaining the Just Price."

But a far better argument for the restoration of the Guilds than Penty or any other sociologist has ever put forward is the fact discovered by Professors Dendy and Whitnell and brilliantly expounded by Samuel Butler in *Life and Habit* that the human body is a federation of independent, co-operative and functional guilds of cells. Thus the quality and responsibility of crafts-manship, the elastic and personal relation between master and man, the one aspiring to be master, the other training him to that end, the religious orientation and the control of exchange, were the organic parts of one whole. There were no "hands" ; there was no marked division between capital and labour, and honest work at a fair price for the good of all was the end in view. The cathedral was implicit in such an organization. And the craft-guild was as integral and local a self-government as the village community. Both were vocational groups, the one of the country exchanging its surpluses with the towns, the other of the town exchanging its surpluses with the country. Neither of these groups are by nature subject to the flux of time or the changes of fashion or the inventions of science or the illusory law of progress or the relativity of economic conditions. They are the organic foundation of civilized man *for all time*, whether in his functional, his individual or his social activities. Every healthy development of civilized society rests ultimately upon them, whether in art or commerce or economics or political theory. If this be doubted, listen to the echoes of folk-song and folk-dance in Bach, Handel, Haydn and Mozart. This is the due and proper explanation

138

of why the intercourse between the temporal and the eternal was symbolically represented in the drama of a peasant and a craftsman, and why the village community and the craft-guilds were dual manifestations, in terms of the social complex, of the primitive natural law. It also explains why, when both of them disappeared, it was not by decay from within but by destruction from without.[1]

It need hardly be pointed out that modern Socialism, which is a State machinery, and modern Trades Union officialdom, which is tied hand and foot to the wages system, are both completely severed from their foundations in the Guilds.

III. The Pillars of Society Pulled Down.

In my *English Countryman* I have already related how craftsmanship in England was all but annihilated by the Industrial Revolution, and how the peasant community was shorn of its self-acting play-pattern, intimately related to its work, by the Puritan Revolution. Next, it was robbed of its individual and communal property, first by the Tudor and, two centuries later, by the 18th and 19th century Enclosures. It is extremely significant that peasant art, stricken a mortal blow after the General Enclosure Act of 1845, and the natural good taste and æsthetic sense of the English people as a whole have never recovered from the Industrial Revolution. Ugliness and economic bondage are sisters. But the effects of this dislocation have gone far deeper. They have culminated in a sense of frustration that has thrown up Hitler, the personification and evil genius of the

[1] In the 15th century the small peasant-farmers and cloth-weavers, with the aid of the manorial lords, defeated the financial ramp to corner the wool-market (*see* Eileen Power's *The Wool-Trade in English Mediæval History*) and made England's prosperity. The Guilds, it is true, did develop some way towards economic oligarchy but not into cut-price competition and bad workmanship.

lower middle classes. They were created by that Revolution as the bulk of the suburban class that has no assured status, nor work-pleasure nor community of interest, and so suffers from the sense of inferiority.

Other historians, Tawney, Hasbach and the Hammonds, have dealt separately with each phase of this suicidal war of society against what produced and supported it, while every history of England at least mentions the suppression of the Guilds by the government of the son of one out of England's pair of historical male tyrants, Henry and Cromwell. But I know of only one historian, English or foreign, whose voluminous pages contain a scattered account of this crime of Œdipus as part of a world-process of social disintegration. I know only one other who takes a world-view of the same phenomenon from the point of view of the resultant exhaustion of the soil. The first of these is A. J. Toynbee's *Study of History* ; the second, Dr Evelyn Wrench's *The Restoration of the Peasantry*—both significantly published in the first year of the present war.

The importance of Toynbee's historical enquiry into the catastrophic recoil of the fate of the peasantry upon those who were the instruments of it is that it is incidental to his main theme. It is not a set piece nor in sequence, and the effect upon the reader is the more penetrating and in the end overwhelming. It comes from the way in which the reiterations of this fate and counter-fate from different angles of approach and at intervals in the course of the narrative steal into the receptive mind.

In one place, he draws a parallel between the twin causes of the decline and fall of the Indic civilization of Ceylon and those of the Roman Empire. Their derelict and malaria-ridden marshlands were a consequence of warfare and the undermining of the peasant cultures linked up with it. When "large-scale cash-crop farming and stock-breeding with a slave-labour force" replaced the "small-scale subsistence farming of a free citizen-peasantry," the *anopheles* made its appearance. To the same dual causes he attributes the downfall of the Hellenic city-states.[1] Elsewhere, he draws another parallel between the decay of the Syriac civilization and that of Orthodox Christendom in the 10th century. Both in fact committed suicide by internal strife as a consequence of "increasing inequality in the distribution of ownership and the impoverishment of the whole countryside," the landowners turning on the peasantry as they did in our own Enclosures. After a gap of many pages, he describes the economic revolution of the Solon régime which gave up self-sufficiency and subsistence farming for specialized production as "a tragedy whose gloom is barely relieved by a brief gleam of sunshine." Once more he returns to the Roman Empire—"the polarization of agrarian society into a handful of magnates and a multitude of serfs" was "one of the mental diseases of the Roman Empire." Thence he refers again to the agrarian life of 8th century Eastern Christianity, "a world of free peasants living in village communities." "This healthy agrarian foundation was doubtless one of the causes of the rapid growth which Orthodox Christian civilization achieved during the next 200 years." But a "sinister change" occurred through the war with Bulgaria in 913. This was caused by the appearance of large-scale *latifundia* following the dispossession of the peasants.

Another gap and he deals in more detail with Rome and the failure of Tiberius Gracchus and his brother to stem the impoverishment and eviction of the Italian peasants by "the new class of post-war planners and ranchers who were able to add field to field by buying up the freeholds thrown upon the market when the owners were mobilized and kept under arms." He might

[1] Cf. also Christopher Dawson's *Progress and Religion*, pp. 65-69.

have added that the theme of Virgil's *Georgics* was virtually an appeal to Augustus to safeguard the small craftsman and husbandman from their eviction by the owners of the *latifundia*. These *latifundia* were stocked with slave-labour which revolted in the savage Sicilian, Catiline and Spartacus insurrections, repressed with an even greater ferocity. He draws a further comparison between the condition of these "slave hoe-men and slave herdmen" and that of the negro slaves on the cotton plantations which replaced the mixed farming of the white settlers in the Cotton Belt of the Southern States.

Then occur these two passages :

> "When the disinherited peasant was first reduced to the status of a seasonal wage-labourer on the land, and was eventually shouldered off the land altogether and penned up in a slum inside the walls of the city . . . the capitalist who was making his fortune out of a slave-tilled countryside displayed as ugly a countenance as his patron-god Mars himself ; and for any disinterested spectator of the joint work of this grim pair of partners, it was not surprising to find wickedness producing results which were morally repugnant and socially disastrous."

Lastly :

> "The revolutionary change from subsistence farming to cash-crop farming and from husbandry to the application of a servile man-power undoubtedly increased for a time the monetary value of the produce of the land ; but the social value of this temporary increase in the aggregate amount of the national income was offset by a concurrent increase in the inequality of its distribution and was more than counteracted by the attendant social evils : the depopulation of the countryside and the congregation of a pauper proletariat of *ci-devant* peasants in the towns. . . . The economic revolution . . . gave the Roman people a shock from which they never recovered ; a shock which revealed its dissolving and

142

debilitating effects in the collapse of the Roman Republic, and in the economic decay of Roman Italy and ultimately in the decline and fall of the Roman Empire."

This verdict by the greatest of modern historians lends an irresistible weight to the famous words of doom uttered by Pliny—*Latifundia perdidere Italiam.* And if these dual passages be followed clause by clause by any reader familiar with the social, economic and agricultural effects of our own Enclosures in the 19th and 20th centuries, he will know that the parallels fit with a diabolic accuracy. The only possible gloss is that the 19th century pauper gang-labour or slave proletariat of our capitalist farming which led to the Luddite riots of 1830 has been replaced in our own time by a machinery which has caused a still further depopulation of the land.

We are led to the inevitable conclusion that if State-owned *latifundia,* as are now proposed, follow the present war, or even if a peasant proprietary is not in time restored, the doom of our own civilization is certain. The true patriot who is sensible of the Christian tradition and peasant foundation of the English nation could but bow his head and murmur—justly so. For he will see in the consequences of refusing the reparation of a great crime-blunder and a return to reality nothing more nor less than the justice of the God whose Son entered the world as a peasant-craftsman.

IV. The Sterilization of Nature.

The link between Toynbee on the nemesis of the dispossession of the peasants and Wrench on the nemesis of the exploitation of the soil is Steinbeck's appalling indictment of the Middle West and Californian *latifundia* in *The Grapes of Wrath* (1939). The book is as raw and crude as an uncooked lump of beef, and an agonizing one to read : I defy anybody with a grain of sensibility to read more than fifty pages at a sitting. But its facts are undisputed. He describes how the tractors were driven through the farmsteads of the family farmers, how they were forced to sell out all their gear at knock-down prices owing to the banks and trading companies foreclosing on them, and the great trek west in gimcrack cars sold them by salesmen bandits. The evicted arrived in California moneyless and half-starved to find that the handbills that had enticed them thither were a calculated trick of the owners of the orchard *latifundia* to employ pickers who would take anything to save their families from downright starvation. All this is a variation upon what happened to our own ex-peasants, the hangings, the transportations, the starvation, between 1800 and 1850. The Middle West lands thus emptied were speedily farmed out by monoculture, machines and no muck to supply *our* urban masses with cheap food and cheap raw material for the Lancashire cotton mills. Perhaps the inner meaning of this dreadful book is summed up in these words :

"And this is easy and efficient (tractor cultivation), so easy that the wonder goes out of work, so efficient that the wonder goes out of land and the working of it, and with the wonder the deep understanding and the relation. And in the tractor-man there grows the contempt that comes only to a stranger who has little understanding and no relation. For nitrates are not the land, nor phosphates ; and the length of fibre in the cotton is not the land. Carbon is not a man, nor salt nor water nor calcium. He is all these, but he is much more . . . ; and the land is so much more than its analysis. The man who is more than his chemistry, walking on the earth, turning his plough-point for a stone, dropping his handles to slide over an outcropping, kneeling on the earth to eat his lunch ; that man who is more than his elements, knows the land that is more than its analysis. But the machine man, driving a dead .

144

tractor on land he does not know and love, understands only chemistry, and he is contemptuous of the land and of himself."

That was how the business philanthropy of the Free Traders worked itself out in practice.[1]

Dr Wrench extends the ground covered by Toynbee but is more occupied with describing the deterioration of natural fertility rather than the disintegration of the equally stable social organism of the peasantry as the result of the impact of urban profiteering upon both. His book (*The Restoration of the Peasantry*) in its turn should be correlated with Jacks's and Whyte's *The Rape of the Earth*. Soil-erosion is the theme of them both, Jacks's and Whyte's from the scientific point of view, Wrench's from the sociological, while the former pick up Toynbee with :

> "The decline of the Roman Empire is a story of deforestation, soil-exhaustion and erosion. From Spain to Palestine there are no forests left on the Mediterranean littoral. . . . No people, however great and powerful in arms, could maintain its virility and dominance under the conditions that must have prevailed 1,500 years ago in the Mediterranean, and no dictator except Nature can restore the conditions that might allow another world power to arise there."

Again, Wrench's version of *solitudinem faciunt* in respect of the Chinese peasant economy, all but ruined by American and European infiltration on one side of the globe and Japanese on the other, should be correlated with Prof. King's *Farmers of Forty Centuries*.[2] Wrench

---

[1] "We advocate nothing but what is agreeable to the highest behests of Christianity—to buy in the cheapest market and to sell in the dearest." (Richard Cobden, quoted in Dawson's *The Judgement of the Nations*).

[2] It is interesting that before that infiltration China was supporting 1,783 persons per square mile to America's 61.

himself supplements Toynbee's interpretation of the fall of the Roman Empire by telling citations from Mommsen. If Egypt, whose annual Nile flood was the secret of its inexhaustible fertility, had been lost, Rome would have starved, to such an extent had the arable lands of North Africa been farmed out for the free bread of the Roman landless proletariat.

This slave-produced wheat corresponds with the cheap imported wheat of exploited Canada, Russia and North America, sold as debt-payments on foreign loans and below the cost of production to make the germless loaves of our industrial city-masses. Wrench makes an illuminating comment upon the reason why our occupation of India, in many respects a truly beneficent if rather stiff-necked rule, broke up the immemorial peasant economy of the Indian ryot. Not in the way of tyranny or greed but simply because the invention of the power-loom after 1760, followed by the flying shuttle, the spinning jenny, the mule and the steam engine and the adoption of the tenant farmer-landless labourer system after the Enclosures had deprived us of experience in the values of peasant cultivation. Adam Smith's principle of unrestricted individual world-competition for wealth crippled our control of the *sowcar* or local gombeen-man who by means of debts and mortgages seized upon the village lands. Famine in India but not in Java where the Dutch colonists preserved the village community with its co-operative tillage and protected it from the exploitation of the moneylender, and so from *latifundia*.

Just as our merchant-revolutionaries of 1650 stripped the peasantry of its cultural skin, so the French revolutionaries destroyed the self-government of the Communes, stripped the peasants of their common rights, loaded them with taxes and delivered them over to usury, while the Communist revolutionaries in the interests of the bourgeois official, the technologist and the urban industrials dealt with their peasants by the firing-squad. All over the world where the natural law of Hobbes had supplanted the natural law of Christianity and of the *paganus* or peasant, the crumb-structure of the soil broke up and in due time was washed or blown away from the excess demands that were made upon it. The great crashes of 1813-37, 1874-1912 and 1920-39 in our own country were experienced on a much vaster scale from the big business farming of the United States whose doom was crystallized in *The Grapes of Wrath*, as the doom of the Hobbesian mechanism was immortalized in *The City of Dreadful Night*. Debt was a harder taskmaster than drought, waste than the utmost rigours of nature. The national greeds for raw materials which expanded the greeds of the combine which expanded the greeds of individual "enterprise" have in North America alone exhausted more than a quarter of a million acres of fertile soil, more than a quarter of the iron deposits, more than three-quarters of the timber and more than half the copper, lead, zinc and oil. In England we waste every year 219,000 tons of nitrogen, 55,000 tons of phosphate, and 55,000 tons of potash as sewage, sludge and house refuse that pollute the rivers and are lost in the sea. Every year the peoples of Europe and the United States pour down into the sea and rivers nearly 20 million tons of nitrogen, potassium and phosphorus for every million of their populations, and every cargo of beef or milk products, every shipload of bones left the exporting country the poorer in the fruitfulness of its soil. The depletion of the Scottish hills drove the peasant-crofter from his starved or sterile home. Australia, Canada, South Africa, Uganda, Kenya, Tanganyika, Nigeria, the Ukraine, the Argentine and other countries have seen their land slipping from under the feet of their peoples, while man who had sprung from the

forest a million years ago is approaching the age of a
woodless world.

I quote from a letter published in a farming paper :

> "One of the worst pages in human history is Man's
> treatment of Nature. First, he took the trees that
> produced the wealth, then he exploited the fertility of
> the humus, and finally turned it into desert, as I realized
> clearly when riding over some of the deserts of Northern
> Arabia. . . . I came to the conclusion that deserts
> were mostly man-made."

The surmise was correct. The following passage is
from *The Rape of the Earth* :

> "To-day, destruction of the earth's thin living cover
> is proceeding at a rate and on a scale unparalleled in
> history, and when that thin cover—the soil—is gone,
> the fertile regions where it formerly lay will be uninhabit-
> able deserts. Already, indeed, probably nearly a million
> square miles of new desert have been formed, a far
> larger area is approaching desert conditions, and through-
> out the New World erosion is taking its relentless toll of
> soil fertility with incredible and ever-increasing speed."

And elsewhere :

> "Misapplied science has brought to the world's richest
> virgin lands a desolation compared with which the
> ravages of all the wars in history are negligible."

The truth is that once contemporary farming starts
"progressing," it heads straight for the Dust Bowl. Man
has played tricks with nature once too often, and, in
spite of the new machines, the average output per unit
area of land is steadily falling. Erosion and deforestation
in the past were of course on a far less intensive and
extensive scale than they are now. Yet the geological
evidence for deforestation as being the true cause for
the abandonment of the Maya culture of Central America
has been recently endorsed by most soil-experts. Aldous
Huxley writes in *Across the Mexique Bay* :

"The clearing of the forest led to erosion, and in course of time all the soil was washed from the fields into the lakes. The result was doubly disastrous : the fields became barren and the lakes turned into enormous mudholes. What had been a garden became a desert. . ."

Only in those little countries like Denmark where the little property-owners still tilled their lands by the law of nature did the soil hold fast, the crops respond to the husbandman, the wheel of life circle from decay to renewal and the sickness of soil, plant, animal and man in serial logic was kept at bay. Chemist, geologist, physiologist, entomologist, botanist, zoologist, agronome, bacteriologist, mechanic, surveyor, statistician and accountant have disregarded or fostered or spent fortunes and lifetimes in vain to arrest that sickness. Only where men thought in terms of goods, not money, of weal, not wealth, of home, not distance, of quality, not quantity, of self-help, not parasitism, of mutual aid, not beggar my neighbour, of nature as life, not atoms, and of God as living, not obsolete, did earth give man his daily bread, and not a substitute.

It may truly be said that small ownership gives man more than quality ; it also gives more quantity than mechanized *latifundia* can ever do. In Germany, the output of the peasant arable farms has been 47 per cent. higher than that of the Junker *latifundia*, of the peasant dairy farms, 69 per cent. In a letter to *The Times* of October 21st, 1940, Sir John Russell wrote :

"We were beaten by the small countries of small holders, and there is no evidence that large-scale reorganization of farming units would increase output per acre."

A few years ago, 9,000 acres of an estate in Montgomeryshire were split up into holdings ranging from 5 to 50 acres with fixity of tenure and economic security. I quote from a report published in 1942 :

"The result in increased production has been tremendous. Where one animal grazed ten years ago, two graze to-day. . . . Where three men and their families lived from the land, there are now nine or ten. Poor pastures have been turned into good, wasted acres reclaimed and new ones taken from virgin mountain-sides. Capital per acre has risen enormously and is still rising. Most important of all, the country as a whole is richer in everything that farming stands for."

Each little farm not only grows an abundance but a great diversity of crops intermixed with livestock and fed on home-grown fodder crops. The small farmers do not actually own the land but freedom from debt and security of tenure bring them next door to it and so to Arthur Young's "The magic of property turns sand into gold." The campaign against small holdings cannot even be justified on the grounds of "efficient" production.

Thus, it is not possible to escape the conclusion that at all times and in all places the uprooting of the peasantry is followed by the decadence of civilization and ultimately by the death of the soil. The conservation of the soil is the indispensable condition for the continuance of man upon earth and the particular values of the peasant economy, whether practised by the rude Hunza on his mountain-side or preached by the bio-dynamic scholar who has read a little in nature's "infinite book of secrecy" can alone preserve both soil and man from "the body of this death."[1]

[1] If the sweeping away of the entire soil in parts of north-western China and the seaming of the land into great barren ravines, chasms and gullies by the floods of the Yellow River from the deforested uplands be compared with similar conditions and causes in Central America, Columbia, Ceylon, Utah, Georgia, and elsewhere, and they again be compared with the flooding of the Tigris and the destruction of its irrigation works in the time of the Sumerian city-states from the cutting down of the Elamite upland forests, it is a tenable theory that the Great Flood of Noah was the consequence of deforestation and the silting up of the alluvial Tigris basin from the soil being swept

V. The Degradation of Work.

The loss of the Guilds and the loss of the peasantry that followed it generated two main symptoms of disease other than that of the degradation of the soil. The one was the degradation of work, the other the degradation of property. Niebuhr has written:

> "Speaking in social terms, one might say that man lost his individuality immediately after establishing it (after the Renaissance) by his destruction of the mediæval solidarities. He found himself the artificer of a technical civilization which creates more enslaving mechanical interdependencies and collectivities than anything known in an agrarian world."

"The machine divorces spirit from the organic body," wrote Berdyaev in *The End of Our Time*. The technician is necessarily the servant of the machine and the master of mankind in a mechanical civilization, so much so that an advance in technics is universally considered as an advance in civilization. This high priesthood of the combustion engine could never have arisen but from a depopulation of the countryside like a river in spate flowing through the centuries, itself due to the destruction of the sense of home which is endemic in the peasant and the craftsman. An industrialism that displaces industry and becomes a value in itself would have been impossible without a contingent urbanism with a materialist philosophy to drive it headlong into further and further excesses of mass-making and expansion. The technician and the corporation, again, are at one in dehumanizing man as worker into the one an automatic operator who mindlessly executes the technical calculations of the expert and keeps the machine in motion, the other into a fluid labour force turned off

---

down the bare mountain-sides. We have only to make the slight emendation from the wrath of God to the wrath of God in nature to be reading a true narrative of what happens when human exploitation sets sheet erosion in motion.

and on the machine according to the manipulations of finance and the fluctuations of the market.[1] The quintessence of the peasant's and the craftsman's work is its variety, the one by the multiple demands made upon it through the diversities of soil, climate, vegetation, growth and their interactions upon one another, the other by the personal supervision of every process from the raw material to the finished product. This direct contact with nature on the one hand and with substance, colour and form on the other has always been and is a mainspring of religious feeling, whereas the total dominance of the machine cuts man off from the world of life, binds him to the inorganic and reduces his personal self to a decimal.

The violent reaction against this degradation of work has in its turn produced the conception of the Leisure State, which, with a final plunge into the very abyss of unreality, is regarded as the potential of Utopia. Already a vast machinery of mechanical entertainment and professionalized diversion has been constructed to provide for this release from the automatism of labour, one form of mechanism coming into action on the cessation of the other, neither having any relation to the other except as the recoil of the one from the other. If it were not for compensating movements like village and county cricket, hiking (in spite of its name), gardening and the country sports, the ballet, bird-watching, concerts, the growth of the county libraries, choice and initiative would have hardly any outlet whatever.

The appalling mirage and atomism of the present Work State and the potential Leisure State are alone sufficient to account for the insanity of the world. In the societies of peasant and craftsman, work and leisure

[1] "When we call the new mass-production system 'automatic' or 'mechanised,' we do not mean that the machines have become automatic or mechanized. What has become automatic and mechanical is the worker." (Dr Drucker : *The Future of Industrial Man*).

were different phases of a single activity and a single pattern of life, the one organically intertwined with the other, but leisure never an escapist device for forgetting work with its consequence that a split between work and play means split personality and a neurotic or neuropathic tendency in the people. Each little cosmos of local self-government provided for its play out of its work and carried into its work the traditions, the incentives, the very subjects of its play. Work, that is to say, was a kind of play, because it was craftsmanly, and play was a kind of work, because it was self-made. And this integration passes through the whole of the animal kingdom, even among the modern man-like bees and ants, so much so that it seems the very law of God. The æsthetic faculty, that innermost expression of man's being, filled both work and leisure, the colour in the flower. The peasant's song was but a variation of the way he built his stack or mowed his meadow; the pageant of the Guild but a new turn of the wheel of creation. Nor, whether he worked or played, did any man, do the job or act the sport but himself, himself in conjunction with his fellows. Such is the antithesis between the self-acting vocational group and the mass controlled either by the self-deified State or the vested interest whether in work or play.

VI. The Degradation of Property.

Except arbitrarily the degradation of property cannot be separated from the degradation of work. Work, that is to say, became degraded as a consequence of the snapping of the link between property and responsibility. The Enclosures which deprived our peasants of their property were a form of absentee landlordism, as the financial trust and the industrial combine are forms of absentee share-holding. The description of how property became divorced from responsibility, rights from functions, and how the gap between them has been steadily widened from the 18th century to the present day, has been brilliantly analysed by Tawney in *The Acquisitive Society*. The economic history of the 19th and 20th centuries has been that of the evolution of functionless property, 18th century expedience in place of principle fathering 19th century competitive anarchy. In its turn it fathered the great congregation of financial and industrial capital that made the division between a propertyless proletariat and over-propertied controllers not only of industry, but, what is even more important, of the circulation of money. Property to-day is no property for the many and enormous and irresponsibly held property for the few.

A farmer who works his own land or a squire who in one way or another superintends it is a functional owner ; the landlord who draws mining royalties from owning land which happens to be coal-bearing or the shareholder who invests money in a combine or joint-stock company and *does no more than* receive dividends on it is an irresponsible owner. Progress has taken the form of the destruction of responsible ownership to the advantage of functionless ownership. Since the responsible owner is more often than not the owner of a moderate property, whether on the land or in industry, recent history has meant the elimination of the small property owner to the enrichment of the large. The remedy, therefore, is not State ownership which abolishes private property altogether but State regulation of irresponsible property and encouragement of distributed property. That was the point of Jacques Maritain when he pleaded for "the diffusion, the popularization" of ownership.

The need of the age is the restoration of property, whether in the workshop or on the land, but responsibly held and co-operatively administered as regional and functional nuclei. In such a society there is room for the 5-acre man and the landlord of 5,000 acres, so long as both in their respective spheres are trustees. "Wealth," as a wise man said, "is like muck. It is not good but if it be spread." The further separation of business from industry and of finance from business has, of course, thickened the cloud-bank which hides the idea of industry as profession or vocation and the idea of property as stewardship. This tremendous drive into an abstract and functionless wilderness is indeed one of the most terrifying aspects of modern Progress. Yet it has been in no sense inevitable. "Industrialism," to quote Tawney,

"is no more necessary a characteristic of an economically developed society than militarism is a necessary characteristic of the national maintenance of military forces."

Labour, says Tawney again, is persons, capital things. How then can capital employ labour? In the Building Guilds, labour employs capital, since industry is a collective responsibility of the worker for maintaining the standard of his profession. This is the link between Tawney's and Toynbee's exposition of the same theme. Individual property, wrote Toynbee, is fundamental for achieving freedom of personality and for controlling the blind extension of mass-production, the incessant output of machines for making more machines. The whole principle of the mediæval ban upon usury rested upon the idea that economic activities were means and not ends in themselves and that avarice was an offence against the property of others. But the formation of profit-making cartels, price-rings, holding companies, financial trusts, banking corporations,[1] investment and

---

[1] "The corporation has replaced the manor as the basic institution. . . And corporation management has become the decisive and representative power. . . . It is no longer based upon the property rights of the individual. . . . In the modern corporation, the managerial power is derived from no one but from the managers themselves, controlled by nobody and nothing and responsible to no one. It is . . . unfounded, unjustified, uncontrolled and irresponsible power" (Dr. Drucker: *The Future of Industrial Man*).

overdraft policies and the like not only eliminate personal
interest in and control of work but even those elements
of risk which the 19th century commercial adventurer
was always taking.

The particular nemesis of functionless property and
the loss of the person involved in it has been indicated
with the utmost point and acumen in R. D. Knowles's
Britain's Problem (1941) :

> "This country is . . . in the extraordinary position
> that whilst its capacity scientifically to produce increases
> daily, its capacity to consume is being slowly but surely
> paralysed."

Again :

> "Briefly stated, the crisis confronting this country
> to-day is nothing less than that of 'money' shortage.
> The 'money' which is issued by the present system has
> no relation to the goods we can produce. And just as
> the loss of his locks spelt bondage for Samson, so the
> loss of Britain's sovereign power to-day (*viz.* of issuing
> money to enable the people to purchase the goods that
> they need) spells financial bondage which takes the form
> of trade stagnation and poverty."

Producing (to use a simple figure) a million pounds' worth
of goods in a given year, the wages system has only half
a million in purchasing power to consume them. The
greater the mass-production of goods, the less the capacity
to consume them ; the more restricted that production,
the more the unemployment. The rise in the use and
consumption of mass-produced goods has been more than
offset by the enormously increased powers of the machine
to produce.

> "Historical fact reveals that from the moment of its
> birth, the machine began to tap out, as it still does, the
> fatal message, 'Increasing power to produce does not
> automatically involve a corresponding increase in public
> consuming power.' That the message was ignored
> mattered not to the machine. And so, ceaselessly and

156

tirelessly, it pursued its task. Gnawing here, nibbling there, the gap between people and goods slowly but surely became wider and wider, and deeper and deeper. With the Great War, the power of the machine to displace labour was vastly increased. And so it was that the pessimism of the early post-war years eventually gave way to uneasiness. By 1931, uneasiness had given way to positive alarm ; whilst to-day alarm has been supplanted by something far graver. For to-day the machine has become a thing of terror. It stalks here and it stalks there ; in the field, through the farm, in the office, in the shop, in the factory, in the mine. And wherever it stalks falls a shadow—the shadow of unemployment and under-consumption."

This is the work of the machine. Yet it is not the machine itself which has been responsible for this degradation since electricity and the internal-combustion engine could and should be of the utmost service in the diffusion of property. It is the machine *in combination* with a predatory philosophy which has degraded work and finally gone on without it, and this is the work of the economic system which has degraded property and has gone on into a functionless finance.

In the last few pages I have outlined, connected and supplemented the attitude of Tawney, Toynbee and Knowles ; there remains for me to correlate them all with the subject of this chapter. When the Luddite Riots of 1811 and the Captain Swing Revolt of 1830 broke up the new machines that *were displacing the labour of the fields and the craft-industries*, they were making an historical protest against the beginning of that process which is ending as R. D. Knowles has described it. But the remedy proposed by him—namely the resumption by the State of its power to issue currency according to the capacity of the people to produce, a power of which it was deprived by the Tonnage Act (*see* p. 104) of 1694—is only a half-way house. The cure can only cover the disease by the sanctification of work,[1] the restoration of the peasantry and a modern form of the craft-guilds. As Berdyaev has written :

> "The restoration of work to its right place in man's life presupposes a spiritual rebirth ; but Socialism is as powerless as Capitalism to save us ; not only because of its economic incapacity but also because of its spiritual depravity."

In other words, the remedy is at once religious and natural.

The rioters of 1811 and 1830 were the dispossessed craftsmen and the dispossessed peasants who represented the idea of functional property and of personal labour of individual quality for the common good. The essence of the Christian idea is the worth of the person and of the old natural law embodied in the Guilds, the worth of the work. Thus, a society which violates the natural law vindicates its truth as indefeasibly as one that obeys it. This law is at once Christian and natural ; it was personalized by the rural Christ, propagated by the primitive Church, sewn into the social fabric by the craft-guilds and the village community, philosophically and imaginatively interpreted by the early 17th century, dramatized by Shakespeare and broken by Hobbes and Descartes. That breakage has led to results proliferating into every social, economic, industrial and agricultural activity ; it has denatured nature, man and the food he eats and it has brought upon the stage of history a being propertyless, homeless, rootless, natureless, peaceless and godless, robbed of his self-determination and debauched by propaganda and parasitic mass-amusement. But because the despair of this being is reaching the limits of his suffering and endurance, he will rediscover the natural law in which God ordains Nature and Man to play a duality of parts, and for the lack of which he perishes. Tertullian said : "Nature is the teacher, the soul the pupil."

[1] Powerfully argued by Dorothy Sayers in *Why Work ?*

CHAPTER EIGHT

ENQUIRY INTO NATURE

I. Shakespeare and the Misuse of Free Will.

IF the Christian definition of sin as the misuse of free will, the self-glorification of the creature and his independence of his Creator, is a valid one, it follows as the day the night that this "sinfulness" is not the heritage of nature. But because this simple proposition is the keystone of the book, it will be wise to have recourse once more to Niebuhr (*The Nature and Destiny of Man*), whose power of epitomizing the Christian doctrine in concise and luminous terms is of sterling service to all who are seeking their way through the Sahara of modernism :

> "The whole burden of the prophetic message is that there is only one God . . . and that the sin of man consists in the vanity and pride by which he imagines himself, his nations, his cultures, his civilizations to be divine. Sin is thus the unwillingness of man to acknowledge his creatureliness and dependence upon God. . . . It is the vain imagination by which man hides the conditioned, contingent and dependent character of his existence and seeks to give it the appearance of unconditioned reality."

Again :

> "One might write pages on the relevance of this prophetic judgment upon the self-sufficiency of modern man, whose technical achievements obscure his dependence upon vast natural processes beyond his control and accentuate the perennial pride of man in his own power and security."

Lastly :

> "For Biblical faith, God is revealed in the catastrophic events of history as being what each individual heart

159

has already dimly perceived in its sense of being judged :
as the structure, the law, the essential character of reality,
as the source and centre of the created world against
which the pride of man destroys itself in vain rebellion.''

This is not a trio of repetitions all saying the same thing
with slight modifications of wording, but a modern
commentary upon Scriptural statement in respect of
man's self-affirmation against God, against nature and
against reality.

In Berdyaev, in Toynbee, in Watkin, in Penty, in
Tawney, in Dawson, and a few, a very few other philosophers and historians of our time, we find the same
interpretation of Christian doctrine, but it is Niebuhr
who most clearly presents this usurpation of the creature
as a triple offence—against God, against nature and
against reality—and its catastrophic consequences.
What is more, Niebuhr contrasts the Scriptural conception with that of the rationalists, the advocates cf causation "as the principle of meaning " and the mystics
who regard the finite world of nature as *maya*, illusion
or as positively evil. It would seem, therefore, that if
there be in truth an inward relationship between God,
nature and reality, there is sound Scriptural authority
for it. That authority is hardly likely to weigh with
the modernists. If, however, their triple repudiation
of all three means that in revolting against God or nature
or reality, they are inevitably revolting against all three
together, their light-minded rejection of the Scriptures
is hardly so impressive.

It has been noted in previous chapters that the Shakespearean tragedy is definitely and explicitly a dramatiza-
tion of this rebellion of the human will, not in hard and
fast terms against God, but certainly against nature
and the order of reality. But that this order actually
is the divine and eternal order, is of the very texture and
pattern of Shakespeare's mind, so that if he did not

specifically Christianize it in name he did so in spirit. Thus considered, and no other consideration is possible, it is an extension and indeed in creative power an enrichment of the primitive and the mediæval "natural law" which was rendered into poetic, philosophical and visionary terms during the first half of the 17th century. Shakespeare's attitude both to evil and the catastrophe it brings in its train was also incomparably more Gothic than modern, while his ideas of free will and redemption were as anti-modern as they well could be. Modern man cannot be reborn like Lear because in his own idea of himself he never sins. As Michæl Angelo's creations equally acknowledge their prime Creator, the two supreme figures of the Renaissance were at one, each by the measure of his own particular genius, in witnessing to the validity of the Christian doctrine of creation. As though to underline his signature to it, the nature of Shakespeare's being was realistic and country-minded.

The claims of the Romantics that Shakespeare was the great modernist have no substance. Because his mentality was of the Renaissance, it follows that the modern view of the Renaissance is a distorted one. Shakespeare shares to the full the Renaissance sense of the grandeur of man—he is the paragon of animals, "in apprehension how like a god." Hamlet who said it was such a man and yet he was flawed, so that Hamlet's praise of man has not the least resemblance to megalomania, the conquest of nature, the Prussian *hubris*. Thus *Hamlet* is in no way inconsistent with the Christian view of man as the creature and yet the *imago Dei*. The *imago Dei* who partially understands nature and himself and so transcends himself and yet the creature bound to the wheel of time. Hamlet's panegyric of man might have been the Psalmist's "I am fearfully and wonderfully made : marvellous are thy works, and that my soul knoweth right well."

Othello was such a man ("for he was great of heart"), though a self-confessed fool and dupe :

> "O thou, Othello, that wert once so good,
> Fall'n in the practice of a damnèd slave
> What shall be said to thee ?"

Coriolanus was such a man, though driven by the sauciness of his pride into self-falsity and self-destruction. Antony and Cleopatra were such a pair, though one a strumpet, the other a strumpet's fool. Timon was such a man, whom *saeva indignatio* drove not like Swift to madness, but to his solitary grave "upon the beachèd verge of the salt flood." Falstaff was such a man whose very flaw is in a sense his glory. In Shakespeare, fallen and transfigured man co-exists and this is the Christian paradox and the Christian mystery. This sense of wonder at the majesty and intricacy of creation and at man the exquisite "piece of work," common alike to Shakespeare, to Traherne and to the Psalmists,[1] is completely foreign to modern thought, which debases man as the product of the Great Machine and exalts him above himself as the law unto himself and the Lord of Creation.

II. Not in our Stars.

The Christian tradition of the goodness of creation and its innocence of human evil,[2] broken as described in the fourth Chapter by certain of the Fathers and mediæval theorists, reaffirmed by the Renaissance and 17th century Baroque art and philosophy and destroyed

---

[1] Richly expressed, of course, in the *Benedicite*, where man is named as part of and within the creation, praising the Lord with the whales and the winds.

[2] St Augustine : "When the will turns to abandon the higher and turns to what is lower, it becomes evil, not because that is evil to which it turns, but because the turning itself is perverse."

by Hobbes and Descartes, the first of the moderns, is picked up again in Dr. Temple's important philosophical work, *Nature, Man and God.* "There seems no doubt," he writes

> "that life in the jungle is, on balance, good. .... It seems clear from the accounts of naturalists that even for them (the victims of Carnivores) enjoyment of life is the prevailing tone and colour of experience."

All who are familiar with the writings of W. H. Hudson, the greatest of modern naturalists and intimately acquainted with the wild life of the South American pampas and forests, are aware of his repeated and emphatic testimony to the joyousness of natural life and the brevity and forgetfulness of its fears when their utility-value is overpassed. We get a notable extension of this view in E. A. Armstrong's *Bird Display* (1942), in which the biological functions of the bird are represented as forming patterns and ceremonials whose very existence is an expression of enjoyment. Moral evil, Dr. Temple proceeds, cannot be accounted for "in reference to the survival of animal appetites into a rational stage of development." This is a perversion of will ; corruption is in the rational and purposive life, in the vitiation of the reason. Not that selfhood is evil but a self-centredness in the personality overbearing its natural God-centredness. Natural lawlessness is a modern misnomer because nature is not lawless, so that the modern assumption of the reason or purpose controlling passions evil by their nature because they come from nature is a fallacy. The need is not to control the natural passions by human purpose but to direct the purpose to right ends.

From this to the acceptance of a sacramental universe is but a step and Temple wisely adds that Christianity is the most materialist of all religions because it does not deny nor denigrate the actuality of the material world. Thus, he lends no countenance to the abstraction of the man of science in separating and interpreting physical phenomena by physical categories only or the sentimentality of the pundit whose illusory purpose is to free the spirit from "the contamination of the material world," regarded as the gross and alien world of mechanical forces and chemical compounds. I may add that Hobbes, the father of the Neo-Darwinian philosophy of nature, who spoke of mediæval scholasticism as "juggling and confederate knavery" is actually at one with that part of it which regarded the natural world as satanic, while Huxley's view of the "Cosmical process" is as satanic as part of the patristic and the whole Puritan view. These alignments are alone sufficient to discredit the futile doctrine of Progress.

The alignment of the contrary view, which is the true traditional view, has in our own time received a reinforcement so much more powerful and convincing than the arguments of philosophers or even the vision of the poetic imagination that it may be said to set a seal of authenticity upon that tradition. That is the rebellion of Nature herself against that predatory conquest of her natural wealth and exploitation of her natural resources presumed by the Neo-Darwinian philosophy to be derived from and so to be sanctioned by nature.

I have already outlined in the last chapter, though in far too meagre detail, some of the effects of this natural revulsion against the modern reading of the natural law; a full account would occupy twice the length of this book. Nature's response to humanity's adoption of her own presumed lawlessness has been the Dust Bowl. It has been the law of diminishing returns, the sickness of soil, plant, animal and man himself, "the desert place" where Macbeth met the witches. And if we examine the actual physical consequences not only of human rapacity towards nature but of our inorganic and mechanical methods of producing food or extracting wealth from nature—the flood, the dust-storm, the plagues of devouring insects, the advance of the parasite, the untenanted wilderness—how dramatically, how terrifyingly they repeat upon a world-scale the convulsion of nature, the *lusus naturæ*, that are communicated to nature from the evil will of Macbeth and of Goneril and Regan and the malady of the world caught from the infection of the State of Denmark! Are not the poet and the prophet "of imagination all compact" when the profundity of insight in the greatest of poets thus emerged as the gift of prophecy ? And how can the Shakespearean vision be regarded as other than realistic when it thus foreshadowed things to come ? Shakespearean tragedy was the catastrophe of the evil will ; it is the modern tragedy.

Part of that tragedy has consisted in the shifting of the onus of that evil will both upon nature and upon natural man. The anthropologists formed an axis with the Neo-Darwinians by detecting in the ferocities of primitive human nature what the biologists assumed to be the laws and processes of wild nature. The Cave Man made a diabolic trinity with the Ape and the Tiger. William James, the philosopher, John Burroughs, the naturalist, and Huxley himself may be picked out as a trinity of modern sages who by incriminating nature and nature's man for the *damnosa hereditas* of civilized man virtually dismissed the latter not only without a stain on his character but almost with a special licence to do his damnedest. For he was no longer *responsible* for what he did. Thus James :

> "There gradually steals over us instead of the old warm notion of a man-loving deity, that of an awful power that neither hates nor loves but rolls all things together meaninglessly to a common doom."

165

Burroughs :

> "What savagery, what thwarting and delays, what
> carnage and suffering, what an absence of all we mean
> by intelligent planning ! Just a clash of forces, the
> battle to the strong and the race to the fleet."

(Apart from the example of intelligent planning
afforded by the German war-machine and our own flock
of post-war industrial Utopias, it might be suggested
that if the fleet win the race, the strong can hardly win
the fleet.)

Huxley :

> "Life is a continuous free fight and the Hobbesian
> war of each against all is the normal state of existence."

H. G. Wells, Tennyson, Winwood Reade in the *Martyrdom of Man* and many others of the wise men have swelled
the ranks of the prosecution. I need not repeat here
what I emphasized in Chapter VI—the profound significance of Huxley thus openly subscribing to the
philosophy of Hobbes.

Thus, the Darwinians and the anthropologists sat
down and wept, not for the crimes of their own age, but
the cruelties of nature that had made· them possible.[1]
It is extraordinary that this morbid and sentimental
moralism in the tone of a whining parson should have
ignored the elementary psychological fact that cruelty
is the conscious infliction of pain either for pleasure's
sake or for some ulterior motive neither of which is

---

[1] When M. B. Reckitt read the manuscript of this book, he wrote
to me—"What about Duguid's *Green Hell* ? " I did not reply—what
about Bates on the Amazons, Belt in Nicaragua, Hudson in *Green
Mansions*, Wallace in New Guinea, all of whose views on jungle life
differ radically from Duguid's. Nothing could be more futile than
such methods of controversy. The earth is earth, not heaven ; the
satanic view of nature from Origen to Huxley conceives it as hell.
The equatorial jungle is not an English walled garden any more than
are the Polar regions, and yet the primitive Sakai and the Esquimo,
who should know more about their homes than we do, are not ferocious,
dishonest or criminal peoples. Very much the contrary. But that
there is a theological mystery about nature I do not deny.

applicable to the animal kingdom. Alfred Russell Wallace in the *World of Life* wrote :

"Carnivora hunt and kill to satisfy hunger not for amusement," and he goes on, "even man with his complex nervous system does not suffer when seized by lion or tiger."

Violent and sudden onslaught in fact paralyses the activity of the nerve-centres.

The very armature of the natural slayer is a natural quality of mercy since it is the most effective means of dissociating death from pain. Animals in natural health and equilibrium suffer very little pain either from death which is sudden or from life which is free from disease or from the anticipation of death which is worse than death itself. What would these philosophic old maids have ? Escape from death altogether—a Kingdom of the Struldbruggs ? Our world being temporal death is the indispensable condition of life. Man does transcend his mortal state, but not by way of these Victorian sobs and groans. Whoso falls foul of death is not fitted to pronounce upon its services to life. It is not death that counts in weighing the values of the natural order, but when and how the stroke falls. Upon the weakly, the sick, the foolish, not, as Darwin said, upon the prompt, the vigorous, the healthy and the happy.

Parasitism is indeed an ugly blot upon the omnipresent beauty of the natural world, but see what happens to the natural sybarite by unsightliness, loss of activity, asexuality, atrophy of limb, slothful monotony of life and dependence upon a chain of outside factors in picking up a living that heavily discounts the chances of it. The liver-fluke, for instance, dies unless an elaborate pastoral drama occurs in the right sequences for its survival. The truth is that man not nature favours the degenerate in nature. Even that is often too harsh a term since symbiosis frequently occurs between host and parasite and only when the organism of the host is out of gear is the parasite harmful to it. There is always a certain elasticity of adaptation in wild nature, but the disharmonious exceptions do prove the rule not of modern rigidity in "planning" but of an order in which a certain freedom of choice, capacity for change and power of development up or down have play.

The Socialist ants, the Praying Mantis that makes a "deintie dish" of its mate with the brains for *hors d'œuvres*, the ichneumon fly, the spider *hungry* for its lover, are certainly striking exceptions. But it takes all sorts to make a world and for a Mantis to be a Mantis is no excuse for man to be a fool, a ruffian or a slave. The point is that very heavily indeed on balance it is a good world, and Vaughan's world is very much nearer the real world than Huxley's; it is rather "a quickness which my God hath kissed" than a "gladiatorial show." Huxley's brilliant qualities and incisive expression did not succeed.in plucking out of him a strand of sheer silliness. "Did he who made the lamb make" the tiger burning bright ? The answer is an unsentimental yes.

I do not wish to overstate my contention. Let there be granted that there are moments in nature's moods, janglings in nature's economy, places in nature's kingdom, ·that turn her lovers pale. Yet I think it could be laid down as a definite law that where and when man acts in husbandly relation with nature, without violation, wilfulness or exploitation, the result is always a virtue and a beauty that emanate both from man and from nature.

As for internecine competition, the Victorian naturalists were writing a history of their own times, not of nature whose spontaneous felicity was known to Traherne but is now lost to man. To contemporary but not to natural man, for the massed evidence of the most recent anthropology has completely disposed of the *a priori* assumptions as to the natural pugnacity of primitive man.[1] Primitive pugnacity, natural ferocity and injustice—it would seem that the more civilized man exonerates himself of his own responsibility for his own pugnacity and injustice, the more, that is to say, he indulges the self-worship of his progressiveness, the worse are his delusions.

III. Nature Acquitted.

Dr. Temple's arraignment of the modern system from the angle of philosophy is supplemented by Dr. Barlow's from that of biology. His *Discipline of Peace* (1942) is an important book because it is the first scientific examination and rejection of Neo-Darwinian science upon its own ground that has hitherto appeared. It covers a very wide field and is a valiant endeavour to show that the future of civilization and indeed of man's life upon earth is something more than a problem of machinery and manipulation—"a little rearrangement of currency, trade and supplies"—and that the mind of the world must swivel on its locked and rusty hinges in order to forestall the impoverishment of nature's bounty and the total disintegration of human society But it is also constructive, not in the sense of a planner's paradise, a moving of the pieces on the chess-board, but of expounding certain principles of reality to which the separatism of science, the divorce of ethics from economics and a false philosophy of nature have blinded contemporary thought. His theme is the organic architecture of nature, that life expresses itself by combination and order, not by power and coercion :

> "Man must become the responsible manager and administrator of Nature. This he cannot do if he persists in ignoring the essential character of vegetative

[1] *See* my own *Heritage of Man*, the works of Dr W. J. Perry and others.

169

performance. If he continues to analyse this under the preconception of a materialistic philosophy, and to exclude all other perspectives upon Nature, he will continue to blind himself to what his situation requires of him. [This is close to Toynbee's concept of Challenge and Response.] The reason why this philosophical method must be abandoned is that it leads directly to the type of economic and agricultural buccaneering which has distinguished the present era and which, we are beginning to understand, is both destructive of our resources and impotent in its attempt to bring order to our societies and comfort to our souls."

The atomic theory breaks down because the vegetative system of nature is seen to be a co-ordinated control of inorganic forces, and the plant disobeys the second law of thermodynamics because it compensates its inorganic losses by energetic gains (photo-synthesis, etc.) and by the discipline of its cellular organization. Life is not itself atomic ; only what it handles is that. I may add that plant-life is the only natural agent against geological denudation, that natural form of erosion which by modern man's rapacity

"is humbling mighty nations, reshaping their domestic and external policies and once for all has barred the way to the El Dorado that a few years ago seemed almost within reach." (*The Rape of the Earth.*)

The plant holds the balance between soil-formation and denudation.

The same organismal correlation and control applies to the animal, replacing its spent energy from plant surpluses. The hierarchical life-energy is thus the reverse of atomic ; it is architectural, symbiotic and co-operative in infinite subtlety of adjustment and balance, and Barlow with much technical detail also relieves genetics of a predetermined heredity. He goes straight back to Darwin and pulls out of the obscurity that Huxley threw over it Darwin's own analogy of natural selection with the cultivation by husbandry of the gardener. Here he walks closely in touch with Sir Albert Howard in respect of soil-vitality and the mycorhizal association between plant-fibre and soil-bacteria, with Sir Robert McCarrison in respect of nutrition and with the promising new science of ecology. Recognizing the interrelationship of all aspects of life from the example of nature, this bold thinker penetrates into the fields of politics, economics and sociology :

> "If man has an organic relationship to the soil and the region, the attempt of propaganda to make his actions fit an industrial system is an assault on his essential liberties."

But something even more vital than his liberties is involved in the attempt of industrialism to dictate the conditions of man's life upon earth.

Barlow's is a difficult book to read and consequently it is likely to escape all but his closest readers that this "assault" of industrialism is also upon man's essential human nature. The *Discipline of Peace* is a crucial book because, though the author does not say so, it actually is a reinterpretation in terms of the most advanced science, of the primitive and mediæval natural law. That too, though he likewise does not say so, is the true relevance and significance of Sir Albert Howard's now famous exposition of his own "Indore Process" of returning in the form of composted heaps all wastes and residues to the soil in avowed imitation of the humus-formation of the forest-floor. Neither Howard nor McCarrison, whose nutritional principles are the rational extension of Howard's soil-discoveries to man's own material well-being, would dream of defining their sciences as expert knowledge of natural processes vindicating the Christian natural law. Nevertheless, they

are so without any doubt, and so in new directions we
are confronted by its fundamental reality.

It is legitimate to go yet further and to see in these
gropings of the new science into the unexplored terrain
of plant-economy, plant-ecology, soil-fertility, nutrition
and the like, an entirely convincing support for the
regional self-government and "old-fashioned" husbandry
of the peasant-craftsman. For what these men of
science wittingly advance as the results of empirical
investigation, the peasant performs both from observation
in the field and by an intuitive sense of natural laws
handed down from generation to generation. His
relation to nature is symbiotic not in theory but in
practice. So the ends of a true nutrition are incapable
of being realized except by the reconstruction of society
upon a regional basis. Was it then a mere accident
that the scene of the Incarnation was a farmyard and
a village carpenter's home ? And is the principle of
depriving modern bread of its germinal essence by
means of the steel roller-mills not a religious and a
natural violation in one ? Charles Marson once wrote :

> "What invisible thing lies behind the cottage loaf,
> the dinner beer ? It has been well said that the generation
> which despises the bread of God cannot get an unadul-
> terated loaf at the baker's, and the people who mock at
> the will of heaven cannot get a glass of ale without
> substitutes. Then this bread and this beer, it is evident,
> are natural and visible signs of some inward and spiritual
> disgrace."

It is needless to stress the truism that the whole of
modern secular orthodoxy in thought, in science, in
character and social organization, flatly contradicts these
modern interpretations of the ancient natural law.
The natural law is above nations and no nation, if it
disobeys it, can escape its judgment. That surely is
the doctrine of creation working in nature, working

through history, but always offering redemption and regeneration through Christ. For some through the natural Christ, for others through the divine Christ, since some forget the God in the Man, others the Man in the God. But the compelling logic of the theme appears to be through God-in-Man.

IV. The Renaissance Exhausted in Our Time.

Nemesis for running athwart the natural law is already in operation both from the kingdom of nature and in the society of man, and no matter what subject be taken nor at what angle the causes of that nemesis be examined, the failure of the modern experiment is seen to be so because it is anti-Christian, anti-natural and anti-realistic. Furthermore, the only binding element that precariously keeps modern Christendom from toppling into a something darker than the Dark Ages are those tenuous links with traditional Christianity that in spite of modern theory and modern practice still survive. In order to realize more fully what this means, it is instructive to glance at the Chapter in Berdyaev's *The End of Our Time* called "The End of the Renaissance." The argument of this Chapter is that the modern world has exhausted the creative energy of the Renaissance out of which it was born. The Middle Ages were not a prison whose bolts and bars were broken by Renaissance man but a school from which he emerged into manhood.[1] His creative humanism clapped its mighty wings in its freedom from that discipline but without as yet taking off into the void, without, that is, leaving its spiritual home, in the broad-based tradition of the Christian and natural law.

This diagnosis is the more trustworthy because it is certainly true, as I have already shown, of Shakespeare,

[1] Dr Tillyard has expressed much the same view in his book on the Elizabethans.

as, much more obviously, it is of Erasmus and Sir Thomas More. But the free play of human forces could not continue indefinitely unless they kept their gravitational centre in the reality of spirit. But this rediscovery both of nature and of man acted as an auto-intoxicant which first found expression in a religious individualism and then in an individualism that had no spiritual basis at all. In so doing, this new man broke the law of his being, for "only the spiritual man, striking his roots deep in infinite and eternal life, can be a true creator."

The exhaustion of the Renaissance took the form of its negation. The bounteous became the regimented life and man made war upon nature with his machines in place of his enchantment and friendship with nature. The joyful diversity of the Renaissance sank into a lifeless uniformity and man who had affirmed his new-found powers with a shout of exhilaration called upon the mechanism of the State to do everything for him. The youthful beauty of life degenerated into the universal ugliness of modern urbanism and modern industrialism. The eager curiosity of the natural sciences was split up into the fragments of specialization. Man no longer wondered ; he tabulated and classified, losing the end in the means. The glorious person became the collectivist and Socialism became merely the reverse side of individual disintegration. The human body decomposed into cubes, men into warring classes. The tradition of antiquity welcomed with acclamation turned into a contempt for tradition as the waste product of the past.

This is a free paraphrase of Berdyaev's chapter, but what it does bring out clearly enough is that the denial of nature and the denial of the divine grace or the centre of human gravity occurred simultaneously, the one intimately related to the other. The decay of life into mechanism equally denied both as surely as determination denied free will. That does not of course mean

174

that the machine is vicious in the act of being a machine. It has become the master of man because it has not been related to a social purpose spiritually apprehended.

The time clock, the stop watch, the conveyer belt, the charge sheet, the bullying foreman, may create an inhuman and purposeless "efficiency" (though it is dubious whether they do even that) but they also generate an explosion of revenge. The substitute for "And God saw everything that he had made, and behold it was very good" became "starve your kids or work my metal." The final exhaustion of the Renaissance is seen, of course, in the Teutonic Power-State, which signals the collapse of the idea of Progress, since the Teutonic State is only distinguishable from the Assyrian in its manipulation of larger resources and its achievement of a greater efficiency. It has no purpose but the "vaulting ambition" of a power yet more extensive and tyrannical and is thus but a satanic end in itself. It carries to the extremest possible finality the Hobbesian anarchy and the Hobbesian mechanism. As Macbeth perished, so will it perish, for the German State is but the story of Macbeth on the stage of the world, though, being but a predatory mechanism, without the imagination of Macbeth. The goal of all deified States is the grave-yard.

In considering the satanic phenomenon of modern Germany, it is necessary to go behind the modern world—to a partial Christianization, to the Thirty Years' War which left a festering wound and flung the peasants back into serfdom and to the unnatural unification under Bismarck. These events have all fostered the growth of barbarism, as have Wagner's music, Nietzsche's and Hegel's philosophy and a hypertrophied romanticism and extremism in thought. This promising bacterial culture was given the opportunity of a fearful development by the modern doctrine of Progress, by intense

175

industrialization and then by great suffering.[1] We are thus witness of an appalling combination between the predatory paganism of the Norse pantheon and the predatory modernism I have already discussed.

The design of this State is to organize Europe into a single industrial Conqueror Nation fed by a ring of satellite nations in a diabolical development of the Victorian economic system in which England was the workshop of the world fed by the cheap produce of non-industrial foreign peoples. Moreover, that efficiency, that regimentation, that extremity of mechanization, are openly advocated in England as the future of England. Detachment from the evil thing is one note, the imitation of it the other on the same trumpet. And a bad imitation because our own State absolutism, being unnatural to the native genius, is an incompetent one. It is the greatest hope for our nation that our recent bureaucracy, perpetually clamouring for efficiency, *is* so incompetent and so corrupt an agent of vested interests. It is alien to the native genius and the native tradition. In our country Socialism is the cure of Socialism. The Teutonic State is what it is because it has de-Christianized and denatured itself more fanatically and efficiently than its fellow nations and the word "efficiency" has in modern times taken on a truly satanic meaning. The father of the Satanic-Teutonic State is Hobbes, not Hitler.[2] By his own words in *Mein Kampf*, "The cruel Queen of all Wisdom (Nature) . . . is bound to the brazen law of necessity and of the right of the victory of the best and strongest"—he confesses so himself.

[1] "The starting point of Nazi political theory was the conviction that the modern industrial mass-production plant is the model for a totalitarian state" (Drucker : *The Future of Industrial Man*).

[2] "The fathers and grandfathers of Hitlerism are not mediæval feudalism . . . but Bentham and Condorcet, the orthodox economists and the liberal constitutionalists, Darwin, Freud and the Behaviourists" (Drucker). And who but Hobbes is the father of these ?

V. The Person, Nature and the Machine.

The nemesis of modernism is not indeed to wait for ; it is in the midst of us. For secular society is based on the idea (derived from Christianity) of the freedom of the individual ; that is its ethos, its ideal and reason of existence. But the decline of the individual has coincided with the growth of secularism and modernism until it has reached a stage when liberty and individuality have almost ceased to be.

But this sacrifice of the individual to the machine has failed to secure its end, which is the subjection of that self-assertiveness *in* the individual responsible for the anarchy of contending appetites. On the contrary, the machine has intensified those appetites, expanded their range and fortified their powers. Civilization no longer has the barbarian enemy to fear from without ; it has, as Toynbee passionately repeats again and again, bred its own barbarism from within,—the "internationalism of the bagman and the swashbuckler." The industrialism which is the living power of modern States *is* the machine and of industrialism self-interest is the motive power. Toynbee, again, speaks of "the aggressive, proud, fatalistic, neurotic life of cities"—how then can the machine be said to have tamed the tiger in man ? The Machine Age has indeed been the theatre of the worst convulsion and hurricane of strife that the world has ever known.

At the same time, aggressiveness, pride and the ideology of the itching palm have been accompanied by uniformity. One obvious example is regional building. The regional cottages, barns, farmsteads and manors of our land are in all their diversity the direct consequence of their fidelity to the region, that is, to the nature of the soil and the particular type and character of the rock from which their materials came. When, however, cheap power, improved transport and full licence to specu-

177

lation came into action and the native was uprooted from the immemorial country to the mushroom town, the new suburbs, the annexes to villages and market-towns and the brick-growths along arterial roads not only became like so many packing-cases but, where they did vary into Tudoresque picturesque, the experiments in the oakery-beamery or chalet or henhouse or battleship or greenhouse style, they portrayed their incapacity to grasp the principles of variation by their studious efforts to achieve it. In other words, they had lost the organic sense of variability in constancy, so that the starvation of the personal factor manifested itself either in uniformity or a pseudo-variety.[1]

The way to the restoration of the West is not, therefore, a yet more elaborate mechanism to kill it. It is an alternative to it and the dual one of the Christian and organic life is the only one there is. There is none other at all. The connection between them—that is the tremendous thing. For if we take the individual human being as the point to start from, we see that a rebirth of faith and a renewed organic way of living are in grain and by their very nature the only forces of life that can master and control the machine, and that control is essential for continuing society in being. The only meaning of democracy is a common son-ship under the Fatherhood of God. Home, the family, local self-government, the satisfaction of man's natural skill-hunger, what Bergson called his innate parochial sense, this has been the social history of Christendom in the flower of its days, and this is the natural life of man. The developmental history of wild nature has been from amœba to man a universal urge towards differentiation, and nature is thus the foster-mother of the individual

[1] Good modern building in the country is almost confined to two aspects : the restoration of ancient monuments and the building of cottages, barons, etc., *on the estate by the squire.*

life of man. What other is Christianity whose God-Man is Person ? Nor, as I have said already, is the true tradition of Christianity one of hostility towards nature and a calm assurance of that ultimate truth is conveyed in the words of Niebuhr :

> "Christianity has never been completely without some understanding of the genius of its own faith that the world is not evil because it is temporal, that the body is not the source of sin in man, that individuality as separate and particular existence is not evil by reason of being distinguished from undifferentiated totality, and that death is no evil though it is an occasion for evil, namely the fear of death."

I have travelled, I think, far enough in this book to be able to make a generalization no longer hazardous nor unverified. A Christianity divorced from nature is not itself and a nature without God only an abstraction. The union of God the Master and nature the apprentice ("Nature is God's Foreman," as Donne said), they are the salvation of man. On a universal scale they sanctify craftsmanship, which intuitively divines the spiritual principle in nature. They alone can lead him from the City of Destruction and take from him the burden of nemesis and catastrophe. For if it be true that the organic way of life is the expression of man's proper human nature, it is also true that his individual selfhood can only flower from the roots of eternity :

> "Except the Lord build the house,
>   Their labour is but lost that built it ;
> Except the Lord keep the city,
>   Its watchman waketh but in vain."

CHAPTER NINE

THE DOCTRINE OF CREATION

I. Doctrine and the Modern World.

CHRISTIANITY is by far the subtlest and most paradoxical of all religions and I am the last person qualified to scale its heights and plumb its depths. Your Absolutes are child's play compared with them. Where I stand in a better position is as a kind of middleman or intermediary between the secular and the religious points of view, my own life and thought having had its being in those secular fields that lie on the borderland between the two spheres and my journey during the latter part of my life having been orientated towards fields more blessed. Not that I can turn my back upon my native self since it became wedded to its native fields of England, nor would I if I could. For my discovery has been not a Newfoundland which spirits more liberated than mine have peopled and still people ; that is not for me. What I have come to perceive is that the earthly fields are a projection of the heavenly ones and that no impenetrable fence walls out the ones from the others unless one chooses to plant it. It is this bridle-path of free access between them that concerns me and of which I am serving my apprenticeship as a surveyor. Perhaps I have not got much further than giving this track of communication a name and tracing back its field-history among the old records.

The name of it is the Doctrine of Creation, one already used by Niebuhr but in altogether too negative a sense. It preserves, he says, "the transcendence and freedom of God without implying that the created world is evil because it is not God." The goodness of creation is maintained both in the Old and New Testaments as God-created, and this accounts for the point and purposefulness they attach to human history. "History is not regarded as evil or meaningless because it is involved in the flux of nature, and man is not regarded as evil because he is dependent upon a physical organism." Thus it escapes both the materialism of mere casuality and the idealism or rationalism of those who sublimate reason at the expense of nature. There appear to me to be too many "nots" in this definition ; it does not positively affirm anything, whereas by its very nature the Doctrine of Creation is an affirmation or it is nothing. There can be nothing more positive than an Act of Creation. What is more, the various aspects and phases and periodic interpretations of the relationship between the natural and the supernatural already handled in previous chapters, however gingerly, are covered by it.

It is my belief that a restatement of the Doctrine of Creation is the only way out of the Egyptian servitude into which the Doctrine of Progress has led the bewildered and frustrated humanity of Western Christendom. The principle of modern Progress, if principle it can be called, is based upon leaving the past behind, ignoring it in its actions, despising it in its theories, misrepresenting it in its histories. For that reason I have attempted to found the possibility of this restatement upon the various interpretations of the Doctrine of Creation mainly in our own past but also at its great source in Galilee. For the successive experiments of the British Church, the mediæval natural law, and 17th century Baroque in all its complexity of expression are themselves so many restatements of this doctrine, each rather more developed than its predecessor but building upon the past, not demolishing it in the idolatry of mechanical progression.

The true mission of modernism is, therefore, a further restatement of its own that will profitably spend the riches of the past, not prodigally waste them under the contemptuous assumption that they are not wealth but dirt. I was talking the other day with the only survivor (to the best of my knowledge) of the old village chair-makers about the former hurdle-makers, broom-squires, bodgers and the like who used to have an acre or so of woodland, and how that they were the true wardens of the woods, far superior to any gamekeeper or conservation society. "Yes," he said, "when I fell trees, I think of the wood as it will be in three years, in twenty-five years and in fifty years." So, just as the craftsman is in continuous relation with the past, in like manner he looks into the future and past, present and future are one whole in his mind. In turning from the past to the future, may his example remain in my mind.

II. Doctrine v. Puritanism.

Not just Creation but the Doctrine of Creation, and this at once raises the whole issue of doctrine. I turn once more, therefore, to the pages of the men of vision which for my own guidance I have frequently consulted in preceding chapters, choosing those who have cultivated widely different fields of thought. What have they to say about doctrine? Dr Temple draws constant attention to Christ's respect for the spiritual liberty of others. He desired none but willing disciples and he formulated no hard and fast doctrines. Credal formulæ were signposts, not revelation, which is "the full actuality of the relationship between Nature, Man and God." The life of faith is no more acceptance of doctrine than the life of the artist is acceptance of æsthetic canons. Faith is not holding correct doctrines but a personal fellowship with the living God which a creed may assist, and without which it is always in danger of falling into idiosyncrasy and that separateness which is the badge of pride and a bar to fellowship.

Niebuhr is even more emphatically anti-authoritarian in his exposition of the cardinal principles of Christianity. An unconditioned moral authority is the parent of spiritual pride, itself the parent of persecution as illustrated in the history of Roman Catholicism, claiming an exclusive and monopolistic truth upon arbitrary grounds that, to say the least, are highly debatable, the individualistic tyranny of Protestantism and the Communist and Nazi despotisms. Religion, writes Toynbee in his pyramid of a book, must penetrate the whole of life, especially the economic system. Faith and tradition are the foundation of Christendom, not an ethical synthesis of progressive ideas. For redeeming our perishing civilization there are certain essentials that the Christian sociologist must demand, such as the restoration of distributed property, the just price, the restraint of usury and individual responsibility, all embedded in the Christian tradition. With them a simplification of life (the word I should prefer to use would be frugality), because simplicity is the release of personality. But this imperative is the reverse of excluding art and culture as a "worldly snare." The natural rhythm of work and leisure as exemplified in peasant society was destroyed as a result of the Puritan conspiracy to exalt work for its own sake. Out of the Toil State has arisen the equally accursed doctrine of the Leisure State. Work being all wrong (I may add), so must leisure be ; get work right and leisure will right itself. Thus modern Christianity has been infected by Puritanism and in so doing has become the left-handed abettor of an industrialism which has destroyed the freedom and joy of living. Joy in nature and the seasonal festivals of husbandry are ostracized

as an obsolete paganism, by which measurement St
Francis himself was a Pagan. This is a free paraphrase
of Toynbee's thought about doctrine, but is not a distortion of his views.

Next Berdyaev: "The Gospel is the glad tidings of
the coming of the Kingdom of Heaven, rather than an
ascetic manual for the salvation of the soul," a rebirth,
not a renunciation. Lastly, I call upon Watkin as a
learned and deep-thinking Catholic. After speaking
of the demise of the Catholic "religion-culture" as a
living organism in modern times, "degenerated into a
commercialized production of lifeless sentimentalities" so
that "the Catholic repository is next door to Woolworth,"
he accuses his own Church of a Manichæism which has
widened the gulf between the people and the artist. Its
dogmatic externalism is part of the same pseudo-spiritual
climate as the dogmatic progressivism of Leftist politics
and the esoteric art-types of the Sitwells, Joyce, Stein
and their kin. Returning to his analogy of vertical
and horizontal, the one representing the transcendental
aspect of man's aspiration towards God, the other the
immanent aspect of the divine permeation of natural
and human life, he claims that the future is with the
horizontal rather than with the vertical. It will be not
with doctrinal authority and ecclesiastical formalism
but with the emergence of a group of new contemplatives resisting the presumption of the self-deified but
godless Power-State, in collaboration with the lords of
industry and finance, to cover all of human activity.
Here Watkin converges with Christopher Dawson, his
co-religionist. This new communion of saints will be
concerned with the free exercise of religion in co-operation
with those lay minds and lay modes of living that are
religious in essence. Its business will be the reinterpretation of the Christian tradition, not the religiosity
of a secular humanism wearing the clothes of religion,

like, though Watkin does not mention him, that of Julian Huxley.

It is clear that these half dozen representative thinkers (and, of course, there are others, especially the sociologists of the Anglican group), speaking for very different bodies of opinion in as different provinces of thought, place and nationality, all come to remarkably similar conclusions. They express a liberal view of religious authority which *is* a reinterpretation of those historical movements in reconciling an outcast nature with her Creator to which I have devoted previous chapters. Just as those movements were a running commentary upon the Doctrine of Creation, so is the work of these separate minds.

Thus, the delicate question arises—what of Christian doctrine should receive a new emphasis in order to restore a Christianity which in a better proportion of faith should embrace both the natural world and the vocational or cultural or organic life of mankind ? The emphasis, that is to say, should be upon the supreme Doctrine of Creation, which includes that of the Trinity and that of the Incarnation postdating the original Biblical Doctrine of Creation but invested with a new, dynamic and sublime reality. This is a readjustment that does not depress the other elements of Christian dogma but rescues those more distinctively creative ones from the moth and the rust.

The Doctrine of the Fall of Man is shown by the force of events to be not so much an article of faith as a platitude. The spectacle of modern political and economic man confirms the ancient dogma without the need of any theological argument. What the acceptance of it does do, as Penty and Charles Williams (*The Forgiveness of Sins*) have recognized, almost alone among modern thinkers, is to remove the myth of the Golden Age from the future into the past which, as the verdict of age upon age has corroborated, is its right place.[1] That, as is evident from my third chapter, at once relates it to the British Church and indeed to the 17th century nostalgia, manifested alike in Vaughan, Traherne, Shakespeare and others, for a primitive innocence, harmony and loveliness. The Doctrine of Progress, derived in this particular from the 18th century perfectibilism that was carried on by the cruder abstractions of Shelley (though not in *Prometheus Unbound*, as Watkin points out), arbitrarily took the Golden Age out of its context and thrust it into the future, where in the planning Utopias it has become more abstract than ever. We have no need of an abstruse theology to argue the validity of the Doctrine of the Fall.[2] Its quintessence is in our own Shakespeare on whom the power of evil was so vividly impressed that it came near to breaking him and certainly landed him for the time being in misanthropy, "as the upshot" (I quote from a letter of M. B. Reckitt to me) "of a failure to find an assured answer to the problem of fallen man after he had rejected the Calvinist one."

III. *Shakespeare and the Sense of Sin.*

I shall return to Shakespeare (who as the greatest of artists does not fit easily into any scheme of philosophic doctrine) a little later when I have shot these rapids myself. What is indisputable is that fallen man is necessarily sinful man, and so devoid of the sense of sin has modern man become that in Germany, which represents the extremes of modernism, he must find a scapegoat in the Jew when his self-glorification does not fit the facts. The consequence of this impermeability

[1] See my *The Golden Age*.
[2] As, of course, it is the basis of free will. "The only basis of freedom is the Christian concept of man's nature : imperfect, weak, a sinner . . . yet made in God's image and responsible for his actions" (Drucker).

is that certain Christian philosophers, of whom the principal is Kierkguaard, have reacted against the fatuity and complacence of progressivism into the depths of a hopeless pessimism. They have carried the decisive words, "If we say we have no sin, we deceive ourselves and the truth is not in us"—into a Manichæan and Calvinist extremity fitly expressed in the title of Kierkguaard's book, *The Sickness Unto Death*. This is nearer the Doctrine of Destruction than that of Creation, and from it we are saved by the contemplation of nature as creation and of all those human activities which reveal man in an organic harmony with nature—in the peasant economy, in craftsmanship and in the creative arts whose modern division in kind from craftsmanship is wholly illusory. Thus, the Doctrine of Creation is bound to bring the consciousness of sin that appears antipathetic to it under its wing, but as servant not master, since despair is as great an impediment to creation as automatism. Creation is not fundamentally the natural enemy of the sense of sin because it is the means to the sense of responsibility in which modern civilization (*see* Chapter VII) is utterly deficient. Without that sense of responsibility for what you do and how you do it, which is the central virtue of craftsmanship, creation is impossible.

This sense of sin is extraordinarily dominant in the mature, the tragic and the prophetic Shakespeare, almost too much so. In Shakespeare, evil is a spiritual not a natural element and this is fundamental Christian doctrine, so that the Christian and the English traditions meet in Shakespeare. Shakespeare whole-heartedly accepts nature, so that his underlying philosophy of life is at one with his native self. Not that the fusion is always perfect. A certain unbalance is seen in the divided attitude to sex manifest in *King Lear* and to a lesser degree in *Hamlet* and *Timon*, in the savage unrelieved cynicism of *Troilus and Cressida* and in the revulsion from mankind in *Timon*. Indeed, it sometimes might be Origen speaking. No close reader of Shakespeare's tragic cycle who avoids both the romantic-idealistic view and the modern, chiefly American, one of cutting him down to the measure of his theatre, can fail to realize that his preoccupation with the mystery of evil came near to unseating his reason. But his blessed English sanity and his profound grasp of the structure of reality readjusted him to the true Christian tradition, so that the dangerous tension was relaxed. So firm was that grasp for all its tremors that it went far beyond the religious conflicts of his age. The whole cast of his mind was intuitively religious and Christian, but to claim him for a recusant Catholic, as is done in some circles, seems to me not only unsupported by any evidence internal or external, but a binding of him within philosophical and ecclesiastical fetters which is a misreading of his mind. There is no systematic doctrine in Shakespeare whatever and he is no Shakespeare who is thus pinioned. And in a curious way this theory invalidates his meaning for us to-day, which is of the utmost importance. For there is no greater significance for us than in the compatibility between his sense of sin and his giant creativeness.

Shakespeare is so often acclaimed as the national poet by noisy tub-thumpers who are without the ghost of an idea what the English tradition is that the reality behind the appearance has been obscured. In Shakespeare, the English tradition, both Gothic and Renaissance and 17th century Baroque, is embodied and in their fusion carried to the topmost top of achievement. He is thus of supreme interest to us to-day when the sham superstructure of the Industrial Revolution imposed upon that tradition is seen to be crumbling and the rediscovery of that tradition is our only hope as a nation.

Shakespeare, embodying that tradition, is our greatest secular revelation of the Doctrine of Creation. And may it be his country sense of home that will call us back home once more to our own land from the wretched gain-getting and cheapness and parasitism and financial cosmopolitanism of more than a century !

He therefore is the bridge that spans "the sundering flood" between the secular and the religious consciousness of England and through him we perceive that the secular genius of the English people, based upon a realistic country tradition and interpreting the natural law with an intuitive appreciation of its fundamental truth, is inevitably religious. Shakespeare is the English version of the Doctrine of Creation. All through the 19th century and the earlier years of the 20th he was an irrelevance ; between 1918 and 1939 he was a back-number, an obsolete point on the horizon left behind in the withdrawing ebb of the national decadence. Now he has become necessary once more to recall us to ourselves.

IV. *The Unity of Nature and Religion.*

Even under the pressure of the severest national misfortune it is hopeless to expect a conversion of any bulk into one or other of the Churches. Apart from the questionable validity of such a movement, none of the Churches is any but a leaky vessel to receive it. What is possible and what is in fact taking place from the successive blows of a bitter experience is the germination of a new sacramentalism towards nature which is implicitly religious and should be but is not inspired and guided by the Churches.[1] For the words of T. S. Eliot in the *Idea of a Christian Society* are becoming more vehemently and desperately true with every month that passes :

[1] Since this was written, it is happily no longer entirely true.

"A wrong attitude towards Nature implies, somewhere, a wrong attitude towards God, and the consequence is an inevitable doom. For long enough we have believed in nothing but the values arising in a mechanized, commercialized, urbanized way of life ; it would be as well for us to face the permanent conditions upon which God allows us to live upon this planet."

To save ourselves we must "struggle to recover the sense of relation to Nature, the recognization that even the most primitive feelings should be part of our heritage." I might almost call this book a commentary upon those words—the "wrong attitude" that took shape in the philosophy of Hobbes and Descartes and is ending in the Dust-Bowl ; "the primitive feelings" that the British Church fostered by its flight from the universal City-State into the wilds, and by its close intercourse with Celtic paganism ; the friendship between men and animals which was a characteristic of the British Church, was caught up again by Shakespeare whose sympathies, as Doctor Caroline Spurgeon has pointed out in *Shakespeare's Imagery*, were invariably with the animal, and again by William Cowper's more isolated humanity towards life, a de-Christianized version of which still exists.

But the converse is also true—that a right attitude towards nature implies a right attitude towards God, and the attitude is being forced upon us by the revolt of nature against the exploitation of finance and the machine. It is a revolt far more widely spread and more subtly operative than its obvious manifestations in soil-exhaustion, embracing as it does the entire inorganic mode of life practised by modern populations. This mode is civilization's defiance of the Doctrine of Creation and because that Doctrine is the truth of the universe it is crumbling in catastrophe. It is the revolt whose messengers are malnutrition, under-consumption, animal and plant disease, human frustration, unemployment except for purposes of destruction, neurosis, world-strife, disintegration and an unreality, the worst symptoms of all, that persistently puts last things first and first things last, industrialism before agriculture, technics before life, acquisition before function, chemistry before nature and the State before God.

It is an unreality that refuses to accept the plainest and most drastic lessons of history. Before the war we had become an *ersatz* people, a seething proletarian or suburban mass controlled by the wage-system and financial dictatorship to produce shoddy or produce nothing, enervated by the clockwork hedonism of mass-amusement, living by the senses from the headline, by the body from the tin-opener and by culture not at all, existing in warrens of derelict industrial cities or along miles of mean or pretentious boxes strung along highways, like racing tracks, upon the face of a country either desecrated or tumbling into wilderness. Was this living, was this England ? We went dreaming on until suddenly we found ourselves in the middle of a human convulsion like the storm in *King Lear* world-magnified. A great deal we had been taught to regard as civilized and progressive we had painfully . to unlearn. The land had to be cultivated, the tin-opener thrown away, the parasitism abandoned, even the financial system that had so degraded us had to be temporarily modified, and the mass-production of trash turned into the mass-production of needful destruction. A rude awakening.

Did we profit by this ghastly exposure of unreality ? We were witness of the monstrosities of the Apollyon State which had gathered into itself the predatory philosophy and industrial habits of a century, and our planners and theorists got busy in totalitarian imitation of it. In spite of the criminal example of Germany, the modern tendency in our own country is to increase the powers of absolutism at the expense not only of traditional freedom but of bare competence.[1] The

[1] *See* p. 176.

191

movement for *latifundia* which history shows to have been the spark which exploded civilization after civilization gained in strength. Yet, though this new arbitrary State showed itself to be still the friend of the financial caucus and the vested interest,[1] an insensate modernism demanded its Leviathan of peace as well as of war. Propagandists talked of "relieving" people of their "responsibilities," not of removing the burdens that had prevented them from exercising those responsibilities. The cry for more and more "efficiency" was for an itching not a horny palm. Pre-fabricated houses were demanded for the countryside as though building a house out of the materials that nature provided out of the soil or rock where the house was to stand were a sentimental dream. And we still thought of saving time in the future when nobody knew what to do with it when saved, and saving labour when the land is crying out for a million more men. Expansion was still the slogan when contraction is the condition of our future existence. The economic spell of beggaring the whole earth to make profits for gamblers and dealers still worked. We went on pretending that the idol of automatic Progress was still intact when it was shattered to pieces, and having neglected our land for forty years we proceeded to farm it out.

But underneath the debris of the old world, a new life began to stir like tender shoots pushing through the litter of winter, the undemonstrative life of the English tradition burst its long sleep, the tradition that in all its variety of forms and fortunes had always been natural and religious both, now tilted this way and now that, but the one never quite losing touch with the other. Shakespeare, that mountain, crowned the landscape of the past ; in Shakespeare the Middle Ages and the Renaissance met and the secular was blended with the Christian mind. Here is the clue to the future.

[1] Viz. 38 of the Directors of the Ministry of Food have "interests" (Hansard) in the milling combine.

CHAPTER TEN

THE CHURCH ACROSS THE FIELDS

I. Church and Creation.

Our task is thus to rediscover the English tradition and within the fold of the Doctrine of Creation. This is my version of Watkin's horizontal or immanent form of the new life which at the same time will be not humanist but theocentric. But if this secular and organic rebirth must be Christianized, because to be severed from essential Christian doctrine is to be severed from reality, in like manner must the Churches become as it were naturalized. It is quite certain that weekly doses of mealy-mouthed pietism or a hash of magic and moralism or a set of stereotyped precepts and taboos that denounces individual pilfering, but is discreet about international piracy, will not only fail to make converts worth having but to be worth anything themselves. Not, of course, by any means that all modern preaching is like this. But there does still cling to the average pulpit that lack of any sense of the profundity and universality of Christianity which in the past made the intellectual and the artist regard it as beneath their notice. In declaring Christianity to be an "opiate," Communism, following Kingsley, was saying a true word, not of Christianity as a faith but of the average 20th century version of it. The City of God is not a celestial Birmingham.

The approaching dissolution of civilization has made it an anachronism that the Churches should regard their duties to God, Man and Nature as fulfilled by preaching against contraceptives and accepting the white bread that causes sterility on their very altars. And

193

the conditions in which such fake-bread is produced—
from foodless, over-stimulated soil on farms in pawn
to banks or speculators and yet further devitalized
by a profit-making milling that puts out of action the
honest country mill, is not this Church business ? "We
have not waited for permission," wrote Charles Marson
in *God's Co-operative Society*,

> "to be thankful for the harvest, we have been thankfully
> and joyfully festive. Why ? Because the people have
> been dimly conscious that the producers and the produce,
> their work and their place in the world, need to be
> considered in the light of the Incarnation. The bread,
> which feeds, has a sacramental value, a place in the
> Faith. It is an outward symbol of labour endured, of
> the skill of a thousand years, the embodiment of men's
> lives."

Everything that offends against the Doctrine of Creation
is Church business ; everything that affirms it, the love
of nature, the craftsman's job, the artist's vision, the
yeoman's husbandry, responsible or creative work of
any and every kind, all true zeal in interpreting that
Doctrine whether by witness in art, by service in honour-
able labour or by devotion in resistance to anarchy or
automatism, those modern enemies of godliness, should
receive the holy blessing. In *The Mind of the Maker*,
Dorothy Sayers has demonstrated that the triune process
of all artistic creation, if authentic, is a fulfilment in
miniature of the Doctrine of the Trinity, as expounded
in the Nicene Creed. That is only another way of
saying that it is the business of the urban clergy to bless
every symptom in the social, economic or political
body which furthers a modern version of the Guild
System in which the accent is on the work rather than
on what you make out of it. It is the business of the
country clergy to bless any movement which aims
at or aids the re-establishment of a genuine rural com-

munity based on distributed and responsible property, not flung helter-skelter over the countryside, but in nuclei ; co-operatively clustered on an estate or round a central farm. The *latifundia*, a propertyless proletariat, predatory vested interests, the wage-system, blaspheme the Doctrine of Creation, and the clergy are the appointed guardians of that Doctrine.

I should say, too, that, as its guardians, they should support not the abolition (since that is Utopian) but the control of the machine, as Penty forcibly advocated, where its use was injurious to the survival of the person, to health, to the conservation of the family, to a distributed property, to craftsmanship and a means to unemployment, to the exploitation of natural wealth and to the mass-production of superfluities. Even so, Penty was too general. Reckitt in *Faith and Society* has suggested that a great deal of field-work is needed to define where and when and how the machine is anti-social. In agriculture, it frequently is so ; it dispossesses the landworker without by any means making for better husbandry. Eliot in *The Idea of a Christian Society* has criticized this "simplicity" of Penty's as Utopian. Simplicity is not the right word ; it is frugality as opposed to the waste of industrialism and frugality is a Christian virtue, while the choice for man has definitely become his mastery of money and the machine or theirs of him. If this Promethean struggle is no affair of the Churches, neither are the words of a philosopher who was not a professed Christian—"We co-operate with God for the redemption of the world." But he takes what he says from a definitely Christian source, for Aquinas cites Dionysius : "It is of all things most godlike to be God's co-operator" and St Paul (1 Cor. iii, 9), "We are God's coadjutors." A few Churchmen and yet fewer of their lay supporters are aware of the necessity for the revaluation of life in terms of the organic because of its indivisibility from religion. But are the Churches as a whole opposed to industrialism, to the disappearance of craftsmanship, husbandry and responsible property? They are united in visiting their displeasure upon divorced persons but is there in any Church a passionate resolve to reunite the severed halves of man's being, the natural and the religious, each withering apart from the other? Until the Churches become aware that the fair price, the social dividend, regional self-government, the family farm, a repopulation of the land, craftsmanly labour and a functional not a State ownership are at bottom religious questions, their inspiration and leadership are except for the few devout null and void.[1]

Christopher Dawson has been careful to warn his own Church from entering into the political arena :—

> "Christianity literally called a new world into existence to redress the balance of the old. It did not attempt to reform the world in the sense of the social idealist. It did not start an agitation for the abolition of slavery or for peace with Parthia."

This is true and wise, but it can easily be misinterpreted as more than the truth. The canonical Epistle of James is a very definite manifesto against social injustice, and where would the agitation against negro slavery have been without Wilberforce? Dawson's own *The Sword of the Spirit* is a society which, like that of the Anglican *Church Social Action*, embodies Thompson's "When their sight to thee is sightless, their light most lightless . . .," while the Papal Encyclicals may be called a modern version of the mediæval attitude to the natural law. Dawson's warning is very timely so long as it is

[1] As a matter of fact, the Churches *are* impregnated with new life, as the Albert Hall meeting of October, 1941, was a testimony. Dr Temple spoke remarkable words when he said these : "I am not myself at all persuaded that the right way to deal with this question is by the nationalization of the land. . . Here supremely the principle of the old Christian tradition holds good, that the right of property is a right of administration or of stewardship. . . ."

taken to mean the non-participation of religious bodies in current political or millennial propaganda. We do not want Grey Eminences in modern dress. Still less clerical support for the collectivist State which must by its very nature be anti-Christian and non-organic. Theology is a living issue to-day ; the future of the Churches surely lies in extending its meaning from the individually moral sphere into the social, economic and, particularly, the agricultural spheres.[1] It is often proposed that country parsons should farm their own glebes. It is vastly more important that they should do their utmost to protect their parish lands as a whole from exploitation on the one hand and the neglect arising from financial pressure on the other. It is not the business of the country parson to farm ; it is his business to protect the land and its community from the kind of treatment they have received and are receiving from the ignorance on the one hand and the rapacity on the other of the town. He should look to George Herbert, William Barnes, Gilbert White (who saved his village from enclosure), John Skelton, Herrick, Hawker of Morwenstow, Chaucer's *povre Persoun*, St Columba and Stephen Harding rather than to Parson Trulliber.

The world needs not a "diffused Christianity" but a truly catholic and creative one with not only co-operation between the Churches but between them and those lay minds who sometimes realize better than they that there are only two sides in modern life, the side of organic and Christian man which observes the English covenant

[1] A good example of the service the Churches can do in resisting the more recent threat to the integrity of the rural community whether from bureaucracy or predatory interests was the protest in 1942 of Canon Williams against the draining-off of village vitality by the Cambridgeshire Village Colleges. Another most promising was the proposal in the same year from the Bishop of Salisbury that Church and farm together should observe the traditional festivals of Plough Sunday, Mothering Sunday, Rogation Tide, Lammas and Harvest.

with Christ and its native land and the machine-made world of the heathen and industrial State. "Our civilization," to quote Christopher Dawson once more, "is passing blindly and painfully through a crisis which may destroy or renew it," and the Churches are being more and more certainly confronted with the same God or Cæsar alternative with which the Roman Empire confronted the primitive Church. The secular State, extending its sway over the whole of social and individual life, will in the end tolerate no Church which refers to another Master than itself. A merely ecclesiastical Church cannot survive the modern world.

From the Christian point of view, says Toynbee, in the very words of the Copec Report on Industry and Property in 1924, "our industrial and economic society is not merely defective but vicious and radically unChristian." Unless religion can restore faith to society, religion and free society with it though against it will perish under the demon's wing of the World Totalitarian State which, so far as it has any goal, is the end of Progress. These are strong words from the historian whose work is like a cathedral for unity, massiveness and complexity. But how is society to be thus reborn ? In three ways only. The first is by successive doses of the gall and wormwood of experience. The extent and variety of modern illusions have a fine mixed bag, the illusion of Utopia, of the "common man," of natural equality, that democracy means no property. The illusion that the application of machinery (State education, for instance) automatically brings light out of darkness. It can but only as electric light. Experience of failure can alone cure us of these illusions. Toynbee points out that Communism, Capitalism, Fascism and modern democracy are all alike in one respect, that they all offer favourable soil-conditions for the growth "of contumelious, beastly, mad-brained war." St Louis, he says, would have been horrified at the ferocity of the religious wars, the Duke of Alva at the ferocity of modern warfare, and a purely proletarian democracy, committed to the illusion of automatic progress and a mere pawn in the hands of a financial oligarchy that has fallen into two gigantic wars in twenty years, cannot escape the judgment of history. It is a democracy that differs from our traditional democracy which, as Dawson has truly pointed out, was "autonomous and pluralist," and, I may add, regional and functional. The concept of democracy has, therefore, through the slings and arrows of outrageous fortune, to be linked up once more with property.

II. *The Recovery of the English Tradition.*

The second way is the recovery of the English tradition, a digging down into the depths of our Englishness. This is indeed the great task of education in the future. In my *English Countryman* I attempted a rough outline of what that tradition has been in its rural aspects, and rural England is our bedrock. Mottram and other writers have undertaken a similar task for the market or cathedral town. From among those many writers who are already recreating the English tradition I would choose one who embodies it in himself, Adrian Bell. He not only writes about the most ordinary things that occur within his own limited experience of his own bit of Suffolk but in the most ordinary way, sometimes gauche, stammering and, as he once said in a letter to me, like a boy at the bottom of the class. Yet the tradition flows through him ; he half talks to himself and half to his reader in a musing recitative, thoughts coming to him out of the air he breathes, his own Suffolk air, intensely homely and yet with the queerest touch of the eternal, severely realistic and yet symbolic, local to the bone and yet universal. His writing is about the most solid, natural, everyday phenomena, and yet it is more like an aroma than anything else. You do not read it but take it in through the very pores. It is an earthy scent, no mistake about that, and yet there is in it a sense of the ultimate reality. As he says himself : "There is enough meaning in the ordinary acts of country life to get the soul to heaven." It is so quiet a voice, an undertone, elusive, like Shakespeare's

> "When the sweet wind did kiss the trees
> And they did make no noise"—

that in visual terms it is not like a bed of flowers in a border, conspicuous to all, this feeling of the eternal, but a shy thing in the long grass, and it often escapes the author himself. He sees the eternal reality in glimpses, flashes ; he does not command the genie, it comes and goes at its own sweet will, not his. It is something more even than England, but the quintessence of England is in it, the England of the wild rose, the parish church, the brown clod. He dreams of an England reconciled both to heaven and her own earth as in her true tradition it always was, for it is the traditional that is the eternal England, not the ephemeral thing of to-day. And there are other writers in our midst who are voicing this fadeless England that we have to rediscover or we are "for the dark."

The scope of an education in the English tradition is almost limitless and extends far beyond book-learning. It is a life-long education, not one ceasing at fourteen, when the pupil is dropped like a hot brick before being pitched into industrial servitude, and it is based on the vocational principle. It is the cultural background to all activities which to-day are barren of culture. Modern knowledge is departmentalized while the essence of culture is initiation into wholeness, so that all the divisions of knowledge are considered as the branches of one tree, the Tree of Life whose roots went deep into earth and top was in heaven. The Danish Folk High Schools are the only European example of a richly integrated and cultural education. It is an education of hand as well as of brain, of how to become an Englishman. It is an education in responsibility towards past, present and future, in citizenship, and in country values. And its vitality depends upon proceeding from the bottom upwards, not from the top downwards, from persons and families, not masses, from the village as the fundamental unit of the nation, not from Whitehall. Educating from Whitehall is as disastrous as farming from Whitehall.

Building up from not preserving the English tradition is our vocation as a people, and the knowledge of that tradition enables us to distinguish sharply between industry and industrialism, money as the medium of exchange and money breeding money, stable prices and booms and slumps, responsible and irresponsible property and the machine as master or servant. It is not afraid of leadership, but it hates control by vested interests and a bureaucracy as incompetent as it is impersonal. "Nought shall make us rue, If England to herself do rest but true." But the Doctrine of Creation is above all nations and all tradition : it is the law of being, and the breaking of it has led Western Christendom with increasing acceleration along the road to hell. The philosophy of Hobbes and Descartes was a defiance of it and subsequent history has been that of its gradual translation from theory to practice. The fruitful movements—the Factory Acts, the abolition of negro slavery (though not of our own wage-slavery), the more humane treatment of children and animals, the discovery of anæsthetics, the cure (though not the prevention) of disease and others like and unlike these, have most of them had issue by resistance to the orthodoxy that was founded upon the philosophical anarchy of Hobbes and Descartes. But before the English tradition became invaded and finally submerged by the case for the abstract and the case for the predatory, the movements injurious to social well-being and individual content—the Tudor Enclosures, the French Wars, the Statute of Labourers, the barbarities of Henry VIII, the 18th and 19th century Enclosures, the industrial expansion following the discovery of cheap power, the rise of the moneylender and others—were violations of the natural law and of the English tradition still governed by the Doctrine of Creation.

For the validity of that Doctrine lies in the junction through it of the natural with the supernatural, of immanence with transcendence. Their "kindred points," when society observes them, maintain its stability and, when society refuses the recognition of them, throws it into chaos. This is not speculation but history, and through it we approach the miracle of the Incarnation from the side of its historical warranty. The teaching of the Gospels was not only "news of heaven," and so of truth, but in the place of meeting between the heavens and the earth sanctified an inviolable truth about the relations of man to the earth. "The men of earlier cultures," wrote Aldous Huxley in *Beyond the Mexique Bay*,

> "were actually aware of external reality. Their relations with it were, so to say, marital ; the world was their wife, and a wife in the full enjoyment of her conjugal rights."

If "peasant," whom progress cannot supersede any more than it can marriage, be read for "men of earlier cultures," this is as good a definition as any of the man of small property in relation with the nature he serves.

The peasant-craftsman in whose society Christ was born is not natural man but the husbandman, he who makes nature fruitful without robbing or exploiting her, who takes the wildness out of her without marring her beauty or wasting her wealth. The peasant-craftsman is the foundation of all culture, of all true civilization, and when the Immortal put on mortality, he blessed the roots of human society. He blessed nature and he blessed man, but in that blessing was implicit the curse of putting them asunder.

III. Alternative to Modernism.

It may appear that I am putting forward only a series of general statements as counters to the dominant abstractions of our times. But if a wrong philosophy is capable of setting a world-catastrophe in motion, the groundwork of a right philosophy with historical warrant behind it, quite apart from the sanction of religion, is the only possible counter. A rival cut-and-dried scheme in a period of plotting and planning is an irrelevance, for modern Utopianism makes no attempt to go outside the terms of reference to the existing order or disorder. The Doctrine of Creation is completely outside it, and the recognition of its truth has nothing to do with Leftism or Rightism and is not concerned with the clash of ideologies. It sees them all as degrees within one kind, of which the Totalitarian State is the finality. The modern as distinguished from the traditional concept of democracy or Socialism is not an alternative either to a dealer's civilization on the one hand or gang-government on the other. All are experiments in secularism ; all are denatured ; none take an industrialized society as other than granted. No organized movement, no class in the community, no accepted school of thought, not even the clergy themselves with the exception of a small sociological group in each Church sees man in relation both to nature and to God in the light of the Incarnation.

So, if we hark back to the 19th century, we see only isolated figures who did thus see him. Coleridge, Francis Thompson, Banister Tabb, Hopkins, William Barnes, Marson and others had to their credit achievements as unheeded as Calvert's and Keats's glowing attempts to rediscover the Renaissance or Wordsworth's lonely one. to recharge the world of nature with life and person or the Pre-Raphælites' to undermine the existing structure with a set of Gothic tools or Maurice's and Kingsley's to baptize the Socialist baby, or W. H. Hudson's to rekindle the sense of wonder of the primitive world. All these were making up stream, not down— indeed most of the Victorian giants were individuals fighting Individualism—but they did not affect its course and now it has reached a vast amorphous lifeless ocean in which creative person is hardly more than an open boat.

But no ocean is boundless ; there is land somewhere and the simile may be carried a little further by indicating certain landing places which seem to offer prospects of settlement in a new country and on good solid earth. The trouble is that these landing parties are often so far apart and out of touch with one another. To some I have already briefly referred. The new organic science of Howard, Barlow, McCarrison and a few others is certainly one, and it links naturally with the very real stir in medical and agricultural quarters on the subject of nutrition. Sir John Orr has repeatedly tried to rouse national apathy by telling the people of England that one-third of the total is suffering from malnutrition. Nutrition is an issue of extreme urgency and if it gathers weight and momentum, as it is likely to do, it will do as much to transform society from bottom to top as any other.

It is in fact the key to local self-government, as local self-government is the key to future regeneration. The whole elaborate apparatus of centralization, distribution and the debt-system which was its motive-power and created a dealer's paradise before the present war, is threatened by it. Be it once established in the public mind that fresh and not only home-grown but locally grown food is the key to health and the system is doomed. Not only would a drastic readjustment of urban congestion and a resettlement of the countryside follow but the modern laboratory attitude to the soil itself would be revolutionized. Once it were recognized that the secret of health goes right back to the condition of the soil and its treatment according to the methods of nature and of a rotational, small-scale (not excluding large-scale) mixed self-sufficient husbandry, the disposal of produce over short distances (viz. to the nearest market-town) has a golden chance of being re-adopted. And if that were to happen, there would be no need to worry any more about the extinction of craftsmanship. Incalculable possibilities hang upon this one issue of nutrition, and when the community as a whole realizes that it spends more on its doctor's than on its food-bill, let the big dealing and distributing interests look to themselves !

The new science is not only realistic and practical with sociological implications. It is opening new eyes to wild nature. In works like those of W. H. Hudson, William Beebe and others, we see science recovering that sense of wonder which marked its first steps in the 17th century. A good example of this heretical science is Gilbert Klingel's *Inagua* (1942) in which profound knowledge coexists with the richest romance and a Traherne-like exhilaration at the glory of the creation. This new school is religious by implication ; professional religion should, therefore, be aware of it. Father D'Arcy in *Death and Life*, arguing for the spiritual reality of the mind, writes :

> "The whole wealth of the universe is open to me, and, if I had the ability . . . I would be able to discover and enjoy . . . most of the secrets and individual glories of this vast world of things."

Inagua is a living witness to the truth of these words.

Intimately allied with the issue of what kind of food we get to eat is that frugality of self-help which is concerned with the whole economy of life built up out of basic needs. This is much more than a mere stripping-away of superfluities which the war has only partially achieved. Superfluities can be graces as well as luxuries. We have been jockeyed by the sudden collapse of pre-war parasitism out of a phantasmal method of existence which not only made no distinction between needs and wants but was paralysing the very nerve-centres of initiative and self-determination, for which the English tradition has been universally renowned. Not even wants came out of personal volition ; by the alliance of mechanism and commercialism they were manufactured from without and delivered the human being over to a paraphernalia of gadgets, expedients, short cuts, pick-me-ups, makeshifts and ready-mades that made doing something for yourself like walking or digging or cooking or using that opposable thumb that first distinguished man from animal, a loss of caste. People drifted from suburb to factory or office-chair or counter like jelly medusoids swinging to and fro in the tidal current.

War, being an evil in itself and modern war most flagrantly so, by no means abolished this atavistic inertia, as is demonstrated by the rank proliferation of a bureaucracy that was itself parasitic upon the occasion and sucked into its non-productive self the vital juices that feed a nation's energy. Yet in spite of it, in spite too of the deliberate scotching of nearly all local endeavour in food-production and distribution, the spell was broken and people had to fend for themselves, to consider ways and means, to become aware of fundamental realities which the tin-opener, the wireless, the motor-car and the movie had hidden from them. Though the process of home-breaking which is the special work of modern civilization was accelerated in one direction, it was stayed in another and the house-craft that was one of the glories of pre-industrial England was amateurishly practised once more. Such measures of necessity and others in agriculture like the resuscitation of thatchers, smiths, basket-makers, those few that were left, the growing of fodder crops, the revival of flax, rye and buckwheat cropping, were, of course, all examples of "putting the clock back," the unpardonable sin of the Doctrine of Progress. Self-help was reborn. True, the ineptitude of officialdom, prepetually badgering those who did the work in the name of that "efficiency" it was the last to practice, penalizing the small producer in the interests of the middleman and "teaching" the farmers how to exhaust their land by overcropping, did everything it could to smother the new-born babe. But the best nurse for self-help is necessity.

The growth of the agitation for monetary reform, the partial checks upon the autocracy of the banks, the fixing of prices (a half-return to the mediæval principle of the "just price") and, of course, the reclamation of the land from wilderness, were other jolts into reality, and it is certain that the usury of imported cheap foods as interest-payment upon foreign loans is doomed for ever. Most fortunately for us we are no longer the workshop and the pawnshop of the world, so that the economic system which lived on scarcity-value, exchange-gambling, unemployment, price fluctuation and the destruction of foodstuffs *together with* their marketing below the cost of production, have received a shock from which it is unlikely to recover. With exemplary clarity and judgment, M. B. Reckitt in *The Vocation of England* has expounded the meaning and potential operation of the Social Dividend, outlining certain dangers associated with it but advocating it as the way to release from economic servitude. By enabling all to receive a sufficiency for the purchase of necessities upon the credit of the productive capacity of the nation as a whole, it would correct the gigantic failure of our economic system as a distributing medium and its gross abuses as a mere profit-making machine. Philip Mairet, in a constructive article appearing in the *Farmers' Weekly* during the summer of 1942, proposed the creation of provincial credit-bodies as a makeweight against the abuse by the State of its monopoly in credit-issue as a result of the transference of the power to create credit from the banks to the State or, better, the King.

IV. The Rebirth of England.

These are all feelers away from the modern *impasse* and in the direction of a return to the English tradition. The natural stubbornness and self-acting heroism of the English people on the beaches of Dunkirk, in cities where hell descends from heaven and in a traditional seamanship among the man-made monsters of the deep, are further indications, in spite of every kind of mismanagement from above, that the old England still lives in the shoddy new. These feelers are one with the thrifty use of the hedgerow and the garden, the struggle for an honest loaf against both State and vested interest, the speeding if not the God-speeding of the rusty plough. None can be rightly called a return to nature or a return to God, still less to both at once. But they are a means to that end and the only means.

They are the laying of the first stones and in the true English tradition, country-born and intuitively religious, and up to the 18th century never radically separated. The more it behoves the Churches to illumine the dimness and unite the fragments of these beginnings.

There is no danger that theologians will fail to stress the doctrines of the Crucifixion and the Redemption. They are less ready to think of God as the Divine Craftsman whose Son chose to enter the family of a village craftsman.[1] A simple creed but of potentialities inexhaustible. There is room in it for the most advanced science but not for a science that confuses the description of phenomena with the explanation of them. The divine spirit enters the spirit of man that makes like nature but sees into the mystery beyond nature. Even to-day the Doctrine of Creation is in our midst, not only in the majesty and artistry of the Universe from which man emerged a free and moral being, but at our own roots in the English village. For every authentic English village is in its trinitarian disposition of church-houses-fields a microcosm of God-Man-Earth, each in profound and purposed relation to the other.

I was talking the other day to a village chairmaker who had made me a very beautiful and traditional yew armchair. He told me he had enjoyed making it because he knew it "would have a good home." The chair was as much a living thing to him as the tree it had come from. What that craftsman said was a line contributed to the universal Drama of Creation. When a man stooks his sheaves at the right angle of incidence, he is not only unconsciously true to the Doctrine of, but part of, the Creation itself. On another day I was looking at an oak

---

[1] M. B. Reckitt has remarked that Christianity was actually diffused by the City-State. But Rome A.D. was a very corrupt version of the Greek original, and was undermined by the new Faith before being blown up by the barbarians.

doorway that opened into a farm-kitchen. On the spandrels under the lintel Tudor roses were carved with decorative streamers. A bench-end in the parish church next to the farm on the green is carved in exactly the same way. The same hand had done for the hearth of the fields what he had for the place of worship, a stateliness given to the farm-kitchen, a homeliness to the church, both the same thing by the same hand—heaven bent over the earth, but earth not left behind at the church-door. When the parson blessed the fields at Rogation, the church was in the fields ; at the Harvest Festival, the fields are in the church. Such integration is true to the nature of the universe. It is this synthesis—religion, nature, craft, husbandry, all in one—we have to rediscover.

Let the church come back to earth—the church in the fields, the church above the cottages like a hen with chicks. For the first church was the Manger and to cut the eternal bond between them is to drift in the void between heaven and earth, belonging to neither. And let the fields come back to the church, looking up from their labour to the tower that rises from the fields. The connection between church and fields has been lost as the connection between work and play has been lost. Just as the right kind of work is play and the right kind of play is work, so the cornfield that has the shadow of the church upon it becomes the "orient and immortal wheat" and the church becomes the Tree of Life, rooted in the earth but its crown in heaven.

"Wait," wrote Adrian Bell in *Apple Acre*,

"and you will see this green England reborn, waking in the cool of the morning with dew upon it ; the sails will stir, the plough and the chisel go forward ; every man in his own sanctuary of spirit, holding steadily to the whole through the detail. In every village there is a monument to the skill and faith of the past. This is the power-house of the future, whence men will draw practical wisdom and integration for what they do. They will rediscover worship. Except for that the whole of humanity would be destroyed."

We pray for that morning, since, when it opens, Christ is born again in England.

THE END.

INDEX

[Compiled by J. W. Meares, C.I.E., M.Inst.C.E., M.I.E,E., M.I.E. (Ind.).]

ABDICATION of the Christian Churches, 13, 127
Absentee landlords, 59, 97, 153
Acquisitive Society, The, (Tawney), 12, 61, 134, 154
Across the Mexique Bay (Huxley), 114, 135
Adamnan, biographer and St. Columba, 39, 42
Æ, quoted, 132
Æsop, 24, 39
Age of Reconciliation, 74 *et seq.*
Age of the Gods (Dawson), 27
Agriculture and the Churches, 197 ; and the machine, 195 ; arts and learning, 48 ; and industrialism, etc., 191 ; primitive, 21 ; Roman, 19 and *passim*
à Kempis, quoted, 70
Albigenses, 113
Alexander of Hales, 65
Alexandria, Clement of, 57
Alva, Duke of, 199
America and Shakespeare, 188 ; early visits to, 48 ; slave labour, 142 ; wheat, 146
Ancient Irish Poetry, 43
Andrewes, Lancelot, 96
Angelo, Michael, 116, 161
Anglicanism, Liberal, 75
Anglo-Roman Church, 45
Animals and pain, 167 ; love of, 33
Animism, primitive, Celtic, Franciscan, 58
Anthropologists and the Neo-Darwinians, 165, 166
Antony and Cleopatra, 162
"Ape and Tiger," 123, 165
Apostasy of the Churches, 127 *et seq.*
Aquinas, Thomas, 62, 69, 94, 195
Aran islands, 35
Archæology of the Anglo-Saxon Settlements (Leeds), 45
Architecture, early English, 67

Arians of the Fourth Century (Newman), 127
Aristotelean realism, 68
Armstrong, E. A., 163
Arnold, Matthew, 110
Art, and Nature, 38 ; of craftsmanship, 131
Arts and agriculture, 48
Assyrian power-state, 175
Athenians, 65
Atomic Theory and vegetation, 170
Attis, Nature-God, 31
Aveling, quoted, 68
Aztecs, 113, 114

BACH, 138
Back to Langland (James), 29
Bacon, Francis, 90, 91
Balder, Nature-God, 31
Ball, John, 60
Bangor, massacre of monks, 45
Bank of England, 103
Banquo, 120, 121
Barbarism and civilization, 177 and *passim*
Barker, Granville, 87
Barlow, Dr, 169, 170, 171, 204
Barnes, William, 85, 98, 197, 204
Baroque art, style, etc., 75, 76, 84, 89, 105, 162, 181, 188
Barrés, Maurice, 49
Basil the Great, 57, 63
Bates on the Amazons, 166
Beaumont, Joseph, 85
Bede, Venerable, 45
Beebe, William, 205
Bees and ants, 153, 168
Behaviourists, 176
Belgic England, 34
Bell, Adrian, 199, 210
Belt in Nicaragua, 166
Bemerton, 96 ; Rector of, 83
Benlowes, William, 85
Bentham, Jeremy, 176

Index

Berdyaev, Nicolas, quoted, 26, 40, 92, 129, 151, 158, 160, 173, 174, 184
Bergson, 178
Bethlehem, 8, 18, 19 ; home of village craftsmen, 21
Biblical Doctrine of Creation, 185
Bird Display (Armstrong), 163
Bismarck, 175
Blake, William, 23, 118, 125, 128
Blaskets, 35
Blessing the fields, 57
Bloomfield, Robert, 98
Bondsmen, treatment of, 56
Boniface VIII, Pope, 61
Bradley, Dr, 89, 121
Bread, germless and sterile, 172, 193
Breage Church, 29
Britain's Problem (Knowles), 156
British Church, The, Chapter 3 and *passim*, 56, 80, 181, 186, 190
British Isles and the faith, 13
Brontë, Emily, 38
Bronze Age on Dartmoor, 35
Browne, Sir Thomas, 74, 89-91, 109
Brythonic England, 34
Buddhism, 72
Building Guilds, 155
Bunyan, John, 29
Burney, Dr, quoted, 24
Burroughs, John, quoted, 165, 166
Burton, Robert, 58
Butler, Samuel, 128, 138
Byland Abbey, 54

CAERLEON amphitheatre, 33
Cæsarea Philippi, 22
Cæsarism, 12, 13, 19 ; Divine, 72
Caldy Island, 36
Calleva Atrebatum (Silchester), 34
Calvaria, monastic, 35
Calvert, William, 204
Calvinism, 95, 114, 118, 186, 187
Calvinist, Huxley as a, 123
Cambridge Platonists, 90 *et seq.*, 104
Cambridgeshire Village Colleges, 197
Capital and Labour, 138
Capitalist farming, 131
Captain Swing Revolt, 157
Carlyle, R. W. and A. J., quoted, 63, 65, 66

Carolingian Empire, 43 ; Renaissance, 44
Carrol, Alexis, 101
Cartesian contempt for history, etc., 109 ; philosophy, 108 *et seq.*
Catacombs, art, etc., in, 28, 57, 133
Catholic Art and Culture (Watkin), 57, 76
Catholic tradition, 97
Catholicism, downfall of, 113
Catiline insurrection, 142
Catullus, 94
Causation "as the principle of meaning," 160
Cavalier lyric, 98
Cave Man, 165
Celtic hagiography and Christianity, 38 ; princes, 34 ; Saints, 58
Celts, Christianized, 33
Central America, 148
Centuries of Meditation (Traherne), 83
Chadwick, Professor, 42
Changeless craftsmanship, 137 *et seq.*
Character of a Yeoman (Overbury), 133
Charlemagne, 43
Chaucer, 28, 60, 197 ; analogy with gospels, 24
Chesterton, quoted, 68, 110, 128
Chevalier, quoted, 38
Chillingworth, 96
Chinese peasants, 145
Chippendale, 136
Christ, a Jew by design, 31 ; as peasant-craftsman, 53, 130 ; of the Trades, 28, 29 ; the Rural, chapter 2 ; the rural Redeemer, 50 ; redemption and regeneration, 173
Christendom, and Christianity, 17, 26 ; faith and tradition, 183 ; modern, 173 ; orthodox, 113, 141 ; western, 11, 12
"Christian" in *Pilgrim's Progress*, 29
Christian, and secular minds, 192 ; doctrine, 159, 160 ; ethos and the peasant, 49, 189 ; natural law, 171 ; origins, 15 ; Pagan Christmas, 29 ; Renaissance, 41 ; social union, 128 ; sociology, 128 ; tradition, 102, 162, 184

213

Christianity, and Nature, 11, 40; analogy between and Nature, 15, 16, 179; both immanent and transcendental, 16, 17; most materialist of religions, 163; patriotic and mediæval, 69; social values of, 128

Christianity in Celtic Lands (Gougand), 38

Christmas, and the Puritans, 31; Crib, the, 30; mediæval, 29

Chronos, golden age of, 31

Church, and bread, etc., 194; and creation, 193; the primitive, 158; social action, 196

Cistercians, and Papacy, 68; Brotherhood, 28; *conversi*, 47; reclamation by, 48; rise and fall of, 52

City of Dreadful Night (Thomson), 115, 117, 147

City of God, 193

City-States, 19, 58, 71, 141, 190, 209

Civilization and barbarism, 177

Civil War, The, 114

Clare, John, 24, 98

Clare Island, 35

Clergy and Doctrine of Creation, 195

Clonard, 36

Clonfort, 36, 46, 48

Clonmacnoise, 36, 48

Cloth-weavers, 139

Cluniac Peter the Venerable, 56

Cluny, Abbot of, 59

Cobbett, William, 128; opposition to enclosures, 20

Cobden, Richard, 145

Cogito ergo sum, 104

Coleridge, S. T., 78, 121, 128, 204; hymn, 84

Collingwood, Professor R. G., 45

Colman and Wulfrid, 44

Communion of Saints, 184

Communism, 68, 193, 198; and religion, 193

Communists, 146; despotism, 183; materialism, 92

Comte, Auguste, 112

Condorcet, 176

Conflict of Religions in the Early Roman Empire (Glover), 24

Conqueror Nation (Germany), 176

"Conquest of Nature," 13, 14, 106, 125, 131

Constable's "Flatford Mill," 136

Consumption and Production, 156

Coomaraswarny, A. K., 136

Copec Report on Industry, etc., 198

Coriolanus, 162

"Cosmical process," 123, 164

Cosmopolitanism, 126

Cotton, 142, 144

Coulton, Dr G. G., quoted, 56, 59

Counter-Reformation, 72

Country and town, 20

Cowper, William, 190

Craft Guilds, 137, 158; and plays, 30; in Middle Ages, 28

Craftsmanship, 67, 179, 187; and Industrial Revolution, 139; and the parables, 23

Craftsmen, 182, 194; antiquity of, 21

Crashaw, Richard, quoted, 94

Creation, its obligations, 6; craftsman as a microcosm of, 52; Doctrine of, chapter 9; 7, 161, 173; Drama of, 209; Man as part of, 162

Croagh Patrick mountain, 37

Cromwell, Oliver, 95, 114, 140

Cronan of the Glen, piper saint, 41

Cudworth, Ralph, 92

Cymbeline, 85

DANISH Folk High Schools, 201

D'Arcy, Father, 111, 128, 205

Dark Ages, 173; rise of the Church in, 33

Dartmoor, 35

Darwin, Charles, and natural selection, 123; "conquest of nature," 13; soil erosion, etc., 170

da Todi, Jacopo, 29

Dawson, Christopher, quoted, 27, 36, 48, 49, 91, 145, 160, 184, 196, 198, 199

Death and Life (D'Arcy), 111, 206

Decline and fall of Rome, 140, 143

Decline and fall of Indic Civilization, 140

Index

"Decline of the West," 11
Decretal law of Responsibility, 66
Deerhurst-on-Severn, 41
Deforestation, 145, 148
Degeneration in Nature, 167 ; of property, 153 *et seq.* ; of work, 151 *et seq.*
Democracy, 125, 128, 203 ; and Nature, 64 ; and property, 198
Demonization of Nature, chapter 4 and *passim*
Dendy, Professor, 138
Denudation and erosion, 145, 148, 170
Descartes, René, 92, 101, 102, 104, 108 *et seq.*, 130, 131, 158, 163, 190, 201, 202
Desert Fathers, The, 33
Deserts, man-made, 168
Destiny of Man (Berdyaev), 40
Dickens, Charles, 128
Dinoot, Abbot of Bangor, 43
Dionysian mysteries, 26
Dionysius, 195
Discipline of Peace (Barlow), 169, 171
Discourse (John Smith), 91
Divine and Natural Order, 64, 100
Dobell, Bertram, quoted, 70
Doctrine, of Creation, 7, 180 *et seq.*, 187, 193; of the fall of man, 185, 186 ; of progress, 8
Dogma, 185
Donne, John, 74, 77, 78, 85, 96, 109, 179
Dorset, St. Aldhelm of, 41
Drucker, Dr, 152, 155, 176, 186
Druidism, 49
Dryden, John, 108
Duguid, Dr, 166
Dunkirk, 208
Dynasts, The, (Hardy), 119 *et seq.*

Ecclesiastical formalism, 184
    Economic determinism, 123; man, 95
Economics and ethics, 169
"Efficiency," 126, 192, 207 ; in human, 175, 176
Egypt and the Nile, 146

Eliot, T. S., 96, 189, 195
Enclosures in England, 20, 28, 96, 97, 128, 132, 139, 141, 143, 146, 153, 202 ; and clergy, 132 ; and the industrial revolution, 28
Encyclicals, Papal, 196
Encyclopædists, 117
End of Our Time (Berdyaev), 151 173
English Church, 96, 97
English Countryman, The, (Massingham), 52, 84, 95, 128, 133, 139, 199
English culture, 102 ; tradition, 192 ; recovery of, 199 *et seq.* ; village, 209
Episcopi vagantes, 48
Epistle of James, 196
Equality, natural, 198
Erasmus, 173
Erigena, Johannes Scotus, 44, 196
Erosion (in soil), 145, 148, 170
Estates, large, *see* Latifundia
Ethelfrid, King, 45
Ethics and economics, 169
Ethne the Fair, 37
European Peasantry, The, (Fordham), 132
Evil in Shakespeare, 187

Fable of the Bees (Mandeville), 115
    Factory Acts, 201
Faith and Society (Reckitt), 100, 126, 195
Faith and tradition, 183
Faith, Christian and natural, 12
Fall of man, 185, 186
Famines in India, 146
Fanshawe, Sir Richard, 97
Farmers of Forty Centuries (King), 145
"Farmers' Weekly," quoted, 208
Farne Islands, 35, 47
Fascism, 198
Faustus, Abbot of Lerinus, 35
Feast of Fools, 31
Fedelm the Red, 37
Fermor, Una Ellis, 109
Ferrars of Little Gidding, 74, 96
Feudal obligation, 68
Flood, Noah's, 150

Florentinus, quoted, 63
Folk-art, 136 ; song and dance, 138
Food distribution, 207 ; home-grown, 205 and *passim*, 207
Fordham, Montague, 132, 135
Forgiveness of Sins (Williams), 185
Fountains Abbey, 54
Freedom and Nature, 65 ; and authority, clash between, 44
Free Traders, 145
Free will, 119, 122 ; misuse of, 159 *et seq.*
French Revolution, 117, 146 ; wars, 202
Freud, Sigismund, 114, 115, 176
Friedlander, Dr, quoted, 162
Functionless finance, 157
Future of Industrial Man (Drucker), 152, 155, 176

Galapagos, 39
Galilee, 31, 49, 60, 130, 181 ; peasant, 18 ; rich in rural industry, 23
Gardiner, Dr, 96
Geddington Cross, 136
General Enclosure Act, 1845, 139
Genetics and heredity, 170
Georgics (Virgil), 142
German State, 125, 175 *et seq.*, 186, 191 ; output of farms, 149 ; war machine, 165
Gill, Eric, 136
Glastonbury, 41
Glebes, parsons and, 197
Gnostics, 69
God and Evil (Joad), 7
God, and Nature, 106; and man, 161, 173, 179 ; and man-earth trinity, 209 ; St Patrick's description of, 37
God's Co-operative Society (Marson), 127, 194
Godolphin, Sidney, 85
Golden Age, 64, 80 ; myth of, 185, 186 ; of Hesiod and Chronos, 31
Golden Age, The, (Massingham), 186
Goldsmith, Oliver, 128
Good Shepherd in art of Catacombs, 28, 57, 133

Gore, Dr, *Jesus of Nazareth*, 22, 24, 128
Gorgona, monastic, 35
Gothic, architecture, 105 ; attitude of Shakespeare, 161 ; culture, 76
Gower, pictures of hunting monk, 59
Gracchus, Tiberius, 20, 141
Grapes of Wrath, The, (Steinbeck), 143, 147
Grave, The, (Blair), 115
Great Schism, The, 62
Great War (1914), 157
Greek city-state, 209
Green Hell (Duguid), 166
Green Mansions (Hudson), 166
Gregory of Nyssa, 69, 101
Gregory the Great, 63, 64, 72, 126
Grotian, 65
Guilds, system of, 67, 137, 153, 194 ; and peasantry, 151
Guild of St Matthew, 128
Guildsman's Interpretation of History, A, (Penty), 137

Hales, 96
Hamlet, 44, 119, 161, 187
Hammond, J. L., 97, 140
Handel, 138
Harding, Stephen, 52, 197
Hardy, Thomas, 30, 114, 118, 119 ; his idea of Nature, 114 *et seq.*
Harvest Festivals, 72, 197, 210
Hasbach, W., 140
Hawker of Morwenstow, 36, 41, 85, 197
Haydn, 138
Headlam, Stuart, 128
Hegel, 175
Hellenic city-states, 19, 141
Hellenistic-Syriac civilization, 20
Hellenistic theology, 94
Henry VIII, 202
Herbert, George, 81, 96, 97, 197 ; his parsonage, 74
Herbert, George, Life of, (Walton), 83
Heritage of Man (Massingham), 169
Herod Antipas, the tetrarch, 22
Herrick, Robin, 98, 197
High Crosses of Ireland, 41

216

Hildebrandine Church, fall of, 60 ;
  Popes, passing of, 62
Hitler, Adolf, 139, 176 *et seq.* ; and
  Hobbes, 176
Hobbes, John, 92, 101, 102, 104,
  108 *et seq.*, 123, 131, 146, 158,
  163, 164, 190, 201, 202 ; and
  Hitler, 176 *et seq.*
Hogarth, David George, 115
Holbach, Paul Henri, 117
Holland, Scott, 128
Holy wells, 49
Honoratus, 47
Hopkins, Gerard Manley, 204
Howard, Sir Albert, 171, 204
Hudson, W. H., 40, 57, 58, 163,
  166, 204, 205
Hugolinus, 65
Humanists, 66
Humanity and *jus naturale*, 66
Hume, David, 101
Hunza, 150
Huxley, Aldous, 114, 135, 136, 148,
  202
Huxley, Julian S., 121, 127, 185 ;
  his idea of Nature, 114 *et seq.*
Huxley, T. H., 112, 164, 165, 166,
  168, 170
Hymn Before Sunrise . . . (Cole-
  ridge), 84

ICELAND, early visits to, 48
  Ichneumon fly, 168
Idea of Christian Society (Eliot),
  189, 195
Idealism and realism, 68, 181
Imitation of Christ (à Kempis), 70
Immanence and transcendence, 202
Inagua (Klingel), 205, 206
Incarnation, The, 64, 66, 68, 110,
  130, 172, 185, 194, 202, 204
India, 146 *et seq.*
Indian ryots, 146
Individualism, 174, 204
Individuality, decline of, 177
"Indore Process," 171
Industrialism, 130, 135 ; and agri-
  culture, 191 ; and churches, 196 ;
  defined, 155
Industrial Revolution, 124, 128,
  139, 188

Industrial servitude, 200 ; state,
  198
Inishmurray islands, 35
Innocent III, Pope, 61
Insurrection of peasants, 142
Internationalism, 125
Introduction to the Devout Life (de
  Sales), 70
Iona, 33, 36 ; communal farms in,
  47
Irish Triads (IXth Cent.), 48
Isle of Man, 35

JACOBIN *droit naturel*, 117
  James, Henry, 108
James, S. B., *Back to Langland*, 29
James, William, 165
Java, 146
Jesus of Nazareth (Gore), 22
Joad, Prof. C. E. M., *God and Evil*,
  7 ; quoted, 7 ; and Christianity,
  8
Johnson, Dr, 75, 115
Judgement of the Nations (Dawson),
  145
Jung, 115
Jus naturale and *jus divinum*, 65, 66
Jus naturale and *jus gentium*, 68
"Just Price" principle, 60, 137, 138

KEATS, John, 90, 105, 204
  Kierkguaard, 187
King, Henry, 85
King, Prof., 145
King Lear, 86 *et seq.*, 106-108, 116,
  161, 187, 191
Kingsley, Charles, 193, 204
Klingel, Gilbert, 205
Knowles, R. D., 156, 157

LAERTIUS, Diogenes, quoted, 66
  Laissez faire, 118
Lammas festival, 197
Landlords, clerical and lay, 59 ;
  absentee, 59, 97, 153
Langland, *Piers Plowman*, 28, 59,
  119
Latifundia and peasants. 141, 142,
  192, 195

Latimer, Hugh, 97
Latin Church, early, 57 ; and British Church, 71
Laud, Archbishop, 96
Law of Nature, 13, 14 and *passim*
"Law of the Jungle," 16, 123
Lawrence, D. H., quoted, 94
Leeds, Thurlow, 45
Leftists politics, 184, 203
Legacy of the Middle Ages (Powicke), 71
Leisure state and work state, 152, 183
Lerinus (Lérins), monastic, 35, 47
Lewis, C. S., 7
Liberty, decline of, 177
Life and Habit (Samuel Butler), 138
Lindisfarne, 44
Local Self-Government, 205
Locke, John, 104, 118, 124
Lord of the Manor, 132, 133
Lucifer, light-bringer and fallen angel, 54
Luddite Riots, 143, 157
Lyrical Ballads, 78

Macbeth, 89, 107, 119 *et seq.*, 164, 165, 175
McCarrison, Sir Robert, 171, 204
Machinery and agriculture, 195
McNabb, Fr. Vincent, 128
Mind of the Maker, The, (Sayers), 76
Mairet, Philip, 208
Maitland, F. W., quoted, 52
Making of Europe, The, (Dawson), 36
Malmesbury, 41
Malnutrition, 204
Malthus, Thomas Robert, 112, 115
Man, as evolutionary product of Nature, 16 ; in God, 173
Man's creaturehood, 6
Man the Unknown (Carrol), 101
"Manchester School," 126
Mandeville, Bernard de, 112, 115
Manichæans, 69, 71, 184, 187
Manning, 128
Maritain, Jacques, 91, 154
Marett, Dr, quoted, 27
Marlowe, Christopher, 106, 107
Marriage, celibacy in, 69

Marson, Charles, 127, 128, 132, 172, 194, 204
Martyrdom of Man (Reade), 166
Marvell, Andrew, 75, 76, 85
Marx, Karl, 16
Masters of Reality (Fermor), 109
Maya culture, 148, 160
Mediæval Political Theory in the West (Carlyle), 63
Mediæval Village (Coulton), 56
Metaphysicals, Shakespeare and the, 89
Metaphysical poetry, 76, 84, 105
Metaphysics, Thomistic, 68
Meyer, Kuno, quoted, 43
Middle Ages, and Craft Guilds, 28 ; and natural law, 52 ; and Nature, 56 ; a Renaissance, 173
Middle West (U.S.A.), 143, 144
Midnight Hour ("Nicodemus"), 70
Milton, John, 95
Mithraism, 34
Modern Germany, 175 *et seq.*
Modernism and modernists, 159, 161, 177, 182, 186, 192
Modern Man in Search of a Soul (Jung), 115
Mommsen, 146
Monachism, golden age of, 57
Monasteries, field labour in, 47 ; become corporations, 55
Monasticon (Dugdale), 53
Monophysites, 69
Montague, 96
Montaigne, Michel, 77
Montgomeryshire "Holdings," 149
More, Henry, 85
More, P. E., 131
More, Sir Thomas, 55, 92, 103, 173
Morris, William, 128
Morwenstow, Hawker of, 36, 197
Mothering Sunday, 197
Moville University, 48
Mozart, 138
Murry, J. Middleton, 133
Mycenæ, 113
Mysticism, 60, 76

NAPOLEON, 119, 120
Nationalization of the land 196

Nativity Plays, 30
"Natural Law," 91, 161 ; in the Middle Ages, 52, 171 ; concept of, 63 ; defined, 65 ; of Hobbes and Descartes, 108 *et seq.*
"Natural Man" and slavery, 63
Natural Satanism, 67
Natural Selection, 171
Naturalists, Victorian, 168
Nature, and Art, 57 ; and Christianity in Milton and the Cambridge Platonists, 90 ; and Christianity in Shakespeare and Browne, 85 *et seq.* ; and Shakespeare, 187 ; and Locke, 104, 105 ; and man, 158 ; as Anarchy and Mechanism, 123 *et seq.* ; as the Great Machine, 101, 125 ; conflicting ideas of, 114 *et seq.* ; conquest of, 13, 14 ; cult, false, 32 ; poetry, 33 ; religious friendship with, 33 ; without God, 179 ; worship, 58
Nature and Destiny of Man, The, (Niebuhr), 72, 81, 159
Nature, Man and God (Temple), 92, 110, 163
Nature-God in folk-memory, 31 ; of Gospels, 25 ; of peasants, 31
Nazianzen, Gregory, 57, 63
Nazi state-religion, 13
Negro slavery, 127, 142, 196, 201
Neo-Darwinism, 27, 101, 112, 164, 165, 169 ; philosophy of, 164, 165 ; view of primitive man on, 27
Neolithic peasants, 27
Newman, Cardinal, 127, 128
Nicene Creed, 194
Niebuhr, Reinhold, 72, 81, 87, 88, 94, 117, 151, 159, 160, 180, 183
Nietzsche, 175
Night Thoughts (Young), 115
Noah's flood, 150
Northmen, invasion of, 45
Northumbria, 45
Nutrition, 171, 204

Ode upon His Majesty's Proclamation . . . (Fanshawe), 97
Officialdom, 207
Omar Khayyam, 116

On Art and Connoiseurship (Friedlander, 162
Organic Science, 204
Origen, 166, 188
Orkneys, 35
Orr, Sir John, 204
Orthodox Christendom, 113, 141
Orthodoxy, 202
Osiris, Nature-God, 31 ; as an ear of barley, 25
Oswy of Northumbria, 44
Othello, 162
Overbury, Sir Thos., 133
Ownership, irresponsible, 154
Oxford Movement, 128

Pagan and secular society, 12
Pagan nature-deities, 71
Paganism, 25, 181 ; predatory and modernism, 176
Palmaria, monastic, 35
Pantheism, 66
Papacy, and Cistercians, 60 ; and power-politics, 59
Parables and ruralism, 22, 23
Paradise Lost, Satan the hero of, 95
Parasitism, 167, 168
Pastor Fido, 94
Patristic Christianity, 69
Patristic doctrine, 64
Pauline conception of primal innocence, 63
Peasant, Craftsmen, 143, 172, 203 ; economy, 187 ; farming, 20 ; folk-memory, 31 ; Galilee and Roman slave-farms, 18 ; poetry of Christ, 22 ; Gospels, 24 ; prehistoric, 27 ; Prince of Peace, 25, 26
Peasants' Revolt of 1381, 60, 135
Pelagius, 37, 44
Penty, A. S., quoted, 124, 137, 160, 185, 195
Pepler, H. D. C., quoted, 50
Peregrini, royal or noble, 41, 48
Père Yves, 93
Periclean Athens, 62, 113
Permanent peasant values, 130 *et seq.*
Perry, W. J., quoted, 27, 169
Peter the Venerable, 56
Pharisees, 24, 87

Picts, conversion of, 39
Piers Plowman, 28, 30, 59, 119, 135
Placentinus, 65
Planning, modern, 168
Plant-life, 170
Plato, 110
Platonists, Cambridge, 90 *et seq.*, 104
Pliny the Younger, 108, 143
Plough Sunday, 197
Poets and Natural Creation, 78
Politics and the Church, 196
Polynesian voyagers, 43
Pope, The, and British Church, 42, 43 ; and natural law, 65
Positivists, 66
Post-Hildebrandine power-politics, 59
"Povre Persoun" (Chaucer), 28, 60, 197
Power, Eileen, quoted, 48, 61, 74, 139
Power-Politics, 72, 125 ; in Papacy, 59
Powicke, quoted, 71
Prayer, Book of, 1662, 96
Praying Mantis, 168
Predestination, 114, 116, 121, 123
Pre-Raphaelites, 204
Primitive Christianity, 56, 60 and *passim* ; human nature, 165 ; man, 169
Private property, 63, 64
Production and consumption, 156
Progress, 175, 192, 198 ; a modern invention, 102 ; doctrine of, 8, 123, 164 ; modern, 155, 181
Proletariat, propertyless, 154
Prometheus Unbound (Shelley), 118, 186
Property, a condition of freedom, 134 ; and responsibility, 153 ; and stewardship, 196 ; degradation of, 153 *et seq.*
Prussian *hubris*, 161
Psychology and Folk Lore (Marett), 27
Puritanism, chapter 4 and *passim*, 28, 94, 122
Puritans, 114, 116, 183 ; and Christmas, 31 ; Revolution, 77, 99, 139 ; view, 164
Pyramid builders, 113

Q*uadragessimo Anno* (Pope), 124

R ALEIGH, Sir Walter, quoted, 24
Rape of the Earth, The, (Jack & Whyte), 145, 148, 170
Raptorial man, 131
Rathenius, Bishop, 65
Rationalists, 160, 181
Raven, Dr, C. E., 99
Ray, John, "scholar of nature," 99
Reade, Winwood, 166
Rebirth of England, 208 *et seq.*
Reckitt, M. B., 100, 126, 186, 195, 208, 209
Recovery of the XVIIth Century, chapter 5
Recovery of English tradition, 199 *et seq.*
Reformation, The, 42, 72, 82, 96, 97, 103
Regional building, a hodge-podge of styles, 178
Regional forces and centralization, 14
Religion and the Rise of Capitalism (Tawney), 102
Religion, and Nature, 38 ; "culture," 184
Renaissance, The, 72, 75, 87, 95, 97, 98, 101, 106, 116, 151, 161, 162, 188, 192, 204
Restoration of the Peasantry (Wrench), 140
"Return to Nature," 78, 79
Revolution, the Industrial and Puritan, 139 ; of 1688, 127
Rewley Abbey, 56
Richard III, 74
Rise and fall of Cistercians, 52 *et seq.* ; of Rome, 209
Rochester, John Wilmot, Earl of, quoted, 114
Rogation ceremony, 57 ; Tide, 197
Roller mills and bread, 172
Roman Briton (Collingwood), 45
Roman Catholicism, 96, 132, 183
Roman Empire, 12, 71, 127, 137, 140 ; and erosion of soil, 145 ; and primitive Church, 198 ; Eastern, 113
Roman *villa-latifundia*, 34

Index

Romantics, 161
Rousseau, Jean Jacques, 116, 117
Rufinus, 65
Ruskin, John, 128
Russell, Sir John, 149

SAINTS of Western World, 86
St Aidan, 39
St Aldhelm, 41
St Ambrose, 34, 63
St Asaph (town), 47
St Augustine, 42, 64, 88, 109
St Bernard, 56
St Bernard of Clairvaux, 57
St Bonaventure; quoted, 65
St Boniface, a backwoodsman, 57
St Brendan, 36, 46, 80, 83
St Bridget, the Holy Mother, 44
St Cadoc, 36
St Chrysostom, 19, 57, 63, 69
St Ciaran, 36, 39
St Clare, 41
St Columba, 41, 96
St Columba of Derny and Iona, 36, 39, 46, 197
St Columban, 39, 42, 43; and Pere-grini, 43; Life of, 42
St Cuthbert of Melrose, 35, 39, 47
St David, Cathedral of, 36
St Finnian, 36
St Francis of Assisi, 29, 30, 184; his sensitive animism, 58
St Francis de Sales, 70
St Gall, quoted, 43
St Gildas, 34
St Hilary, 57
St Hildegarde, 85
St Illtyd, 36
St Irenæus, 63
St Kentigern, 47
St Kevin, 38
St Louis, 198
St Maelduth, 41
St Morwenna, 37, 41
St Motacilla, 41
St Patrick, 37, 47; origin and career of, 34
St Paul, 64, 110, 195
St Samson, 36
St Satyrus, 57
St Teresa, 94

St Thierry monastery, 49
St Theodulph the Ploughman, 49, 54
St Thomas Aquinas (Chesterton), 68
St Walaric, 49
Satanic natural world, 164; Teutonic State, 176; view of Nature, 166
Satire on Man (Rochester), 114
Sayers, Dorothy L., 76, 158, 194
Science, and religion, 105; beginning of, 77
Science and the Modern World (Whitehead), 101
Scottish crofters, 147
Self-government, 134
Seventeenth Century Background (Willey), 69, 77, 104
Shakespeare, 74, 82, 83, 95, 96, 106, 107, 110, 115, 158, 160, 161, 162, 165, 173, 186, 192, 200; and misuse of Free Will, 159 et seq.; and the Sense of Sin, 186 et seq.; his idea of Nature, 114 et seq.; the rural, 22
Shakespearean Tragedy (Bradley), 121
Shakespeare's Imagery (Spurgeon), 107, 190
Shavian life-process, 66; vitalism, 116
Shaw, George Bernard, 66
Shelley, P. B., 105, 118, 186
Sickness Unto Death, The, (Kierkguaard), 187
Silchester amphitheatre, 33; basilica in, 34, 42
Sin, Christian definition of, 159; consciousness of, 187
Skellig Michael, monastic cells in, 35
Skelton, John, 197
Slave labour, 19, 141, 142; of Rome, 19
Slavery, negro, 127, 142, 196, 201
Slavery, "contrary to Nature," 63
Small holdings, 149 et seq.
Smith, Adam, 112, 115, 124, 125, 146
Smith, John, discourse, 91, 92
Smith, Sydney, "squarson," 59

Social and Political Ideas of Some Great Mediæval Thinkers, The, (Aveling), 68
Social Contract (Rousseau), 117
Social Dividend, 208
Socialism, 139, 158, 174, 203 ; and Individualism, 7
Soil, erosion, 145, 148, 170 ; vitality, 171 *et seq.*
Song to David (Smart), 84
Spartacus insurrection, 142
Spengler's idea of Nature, 114 *et seq.*
Spinning jenny, 146
Spiritual freedom and material force, 62
Spiritual man, 174
Spurgeon, Dr Caroline, 107, 190
Squire and peasant, 134
State, absolutism, 95, 176 ; absolutism and capitalism, 125 ; collectivist, 197 ; the deified, 66 ; industrial and secular, 198 ; ownership and regulation, 154 ; toil and leisure, 183
Statute of Labourers, 202
Steam engine, invention of, 146
Steinbeck, John, 143, 147
Stoics, 61, 66
Stone circles, 36
Stuarts and Cromwell, 114
Study of History (Toynbee), 19, 26, 44, 50, 61, 62, 113, 140
Sumerian city-states, 150
Sunday, Plough and Mothering, 197
Supply and Demand, Law of, 122, 126
"Survival of the fittest," 124
Swift, Dean, 115, 162
Sword of the Spirit, The, (Dawson), 196
Symbiosis, host and parasite, 168 of land and people, 14
Synod of Whitby, 42
Synthesis of religion and nature, etc., 210
Syriac civilization, 141

Tabb, Banister, 204
Tammuz, Nature-God, 31
Tawney, R. H. (*The Acquisitive Society*), quoted, 12, 13, 61, 66, 102, 104, 118, 127, 134, 140, 154, 155, 157, 160
Taylor, Jeremy, 70, 83, 96
Tempest, The, 85
Temple, Dr, 92, 110, 128, 163, 169, 182, 196
Tennyson, Alfred, Lord, 166
Tertullian, quoted, 25, 158
Tess of the D'Urbevilles (Hardy), 119
Teutonic Power-State, 175 *et seq.*
Theology, Pauline and Augustinian 69
Thompson, Francis, 76, 196, 204
Thoreau, Henry David, 46
Timon of Athens, 162, 187, 188
Tintern Abbey, 54
Tonnage Act, 1694, 103, 104, 157
Totalitarian States, 62, 102, 176, 191, 203
Tournai, Stephen of, 65
Town and country, clash between, 44
Town Guilds, 133
Toynbee, Dr A. J., 19, 26, 44, 50, 61, 62, 105, 113, 116, 126, 140, 143, 145, 155, 157, 160, 170, 177, 183, 184, 198
Tractarians, 128
Trades Unionism, 139
Traditional England, 200
Tradition and Modernism (Penty), 124
Traherne, Bertram Dobell, quoted, 26, 70, 74, 77, 83, 84, 109, 162, 168, 186, 205
Troilus and Cressida, 188
Tudors and Tudor enclosures, 96, 103, 139

Unemployment and the machine, 157
Unity of Nature and Religion, 189 *et seq.*
Urbanism, modern, 136, 174
Usury, 155, 183 ; Papal denunciation of, 60
Utopia, 129, 152, 166, 186, 195, 198, 203

VALUES, Christian and Natural, 15
Vaughan, Henry, the Silurist, 79 *et seq.*; quoted, 27, 83, 106, 107, 109, 129, 168, 186
Vellum painting, etc., 48
Vested interests, 176, 192, 195
Victorian conventions, 122; economics, 176; giants, 204; naturalists, 168
Virgil, 142
Vita Columbani, 39
Vita Davidis, 47
Vitæ Sanctorum Hiberniæ, 38
Vocation of England, The, (Reckitt), 208

WADDELL, Helen, quoted, 33, 38
Wage-system, 195
Wagner, Richard, 175
Wakefield Cycle Plays, 30
Wallace, Alfred Russell, 166, 167
Walton, Isaac, 58, 83
War, causes of, 198; religious and economic, 62
Watkin, E. I., quoted, 57, 76, 84, 116, 160, 184-86, 193
Wealth, and riches, 182; real and artificial standards of, 7
Wealth of Nations (Smith), 124
Weekly Review, quoted, 50
Wells, H. G., 115, 166
Wesley, John, 128
Wessex, 122
West Chillington, 29
Western Christendom, 11, 12, 37, 102, 181, 201
Western civilization, decline of, 15
Westcott, Brooke Foss, 128
Western Europe in the Middle Ages, 62
Wheat-germ and grain, 26
Whichcote, Benjamin, 92
White, Gilbert, 197

Whitehead, Professor, 101
Whitman, Walt, 106, 108
Whitnell, Professor, 138
Why Work (Sayers), 158
Widdrington, Canon P. E. T., 128
Wilberforce, Canon, 196
Willey, Basil, quoted, 69, 77, 90 *et seq.*, 104, 105, 109
Williams, Charles, quoted, 86, 185
Williams, Canon, 197
Winter's Tale, The, 85
Witches (of *Macbeth*), 74, 119, 120
Wool, and Cistercians, 54, 55; market cornering of, 139; trade, attempt to corner, 61
Wool-Trade in English Mediæval History, The, (Power), 139
Wordsworth, Dorothy, 40, 45
Wordsworth, William, 78, 80, 90, 98, 109, 204
Work, and leisure, 183; degradation of, 151 *et seq.*
World of Life (Wallace), 167
Work State and Leisure State, 152
Wren, Sir Christopher, 105
Wrench, Evelyn, 140, 143, 145, 146
Wulfrid and the King, 44

YARNTON village, 56
Yellow River erosion, 150
Yeomen, 75, 99
York Cycle Plays, 30
Yorkshire Cistercians, 48
Young, Arthur, 115, 150
Yule Log, Yule Firth and Yule Tree, 31

ZAGREUS, Nature-God, 31
Zealot, 27
Zoomorphic decoration, 41